Autism

by Peggy J. Parks

Current Issues

ReferencePoint
Press™

San Diego, CA

© 2009 ReferencePoint Press, Inc.

For more information, contact:
ReferencePoint Press, Inc.
PO Box 27779
San Diego, CA 92198
www.ReferencePointPress.com

Picture credits:
Steve Zmina: 33–36, 50–53, 67–70, 83–85
AP Images: 13, 15

Parks, Peggy J., 1951–
   Autism / by Peggy J. Parks.
     p. cm.—(Compact research)
   Includes bibliographical references and index.
   ISBN-13: 978-1-60152-058-6 (hardback)
   ISBN-10: 1-60152-058-1 (hardback)
   1. Autism. I. Title.
   RC553.A88P375 2008
   616.85'882—dc22
                                                     2008021335

Contents

Foreword

As modern civilization continues to evolve, its ability to create, store, distribute, and access information expands exponentially. The explosion of information from all media continues to increase at a phenomenal rate. By 2020 some experts predict the worldwide information base will double every 73 days. While access to diverse sources of information and perspectives is paramount to any democratic society, information alone cannot help people gain knowledge and understanding. Information must be organized and presented clearly and succinctly in order to be understood. The challenge in the digital age becomes not the creation of information, but how best to sort, organize, enhance, and present information.

ReferencePoint Press developed the *Compact Research* series with this challenge of the information age in mind. More than any other subject area today, researching current issues can yield vast, diverse, and unqualified information that can be intimidating and overwhelming for even the most advanced and motivated researcher. The *Compact Research* series offers a compact, relevant, intelligent, and conveniently organized collection of information covering a variety of current topics ranging from illegal immigration and methamphetamine to diseases such as anorexia and meningitis.

The series focuses on three types of information: objective single-author narratives, opinion-based primary source quotations, and facts and statistics. The clearly written objective narratives provide context and reliable background information. Primary source quotes are carefully selected and cited, exposing the reader to differing points of view. And facts and statistics sections aid the reader in evaluating perspectives. Presenting these key types of information creates a richer, more balanced learning experience.

For better understanding and convenience, the series enhances information by organizing it into narrower topics and adding design features that make it easy for a reader to identify desired content. For example, in *Compact Research: Illegal Immigration*, a chapter covering the economic impact of illegal immigration has an objective narrative explaining the various ways the economy is impacted, a balanced section of numerous primary source quotes on the topic, followed by facts and full-color illustrations to encourage evaluation of contrasting perspectives.

The ancient Roman philosopher Lucius Annaeus Seneca wrote, "It is quality rather than quantity that matters." More than just a collection of content, the *Compact Research* series is simply committed to creating, finding, organizing, and presenting the most relevant and appropriate amount of information on a current topic in a user-friendly style that invites, intrigues, and fosters understanding.

Autism at a Glance

What It Is

Autism is a complex disorder that affects the brain's normal development of social and communication skills.

Prevalence

Autism affects an estimated 1 out of every 150 children in the United States.

Causes

Although its exact cause is unknown, most scientists believe that autism is caused by a combination of genetic and environmental factors.

Controversy

Thousands of parents, as well as some doctors and scientists, believe that autism is triggered by childhood vaccines.

Symptoms

Common autistic traits are an inability to make eye contact, cuddle, and respond when spoken to. Others are lining up toys rather than playing with them, flapping arms, twirling in circles, incessant humming, and walking on toes.

Diagnosis

There is no medical test that can diagnose autism. A comprehensive evaluation typically includes clinical observations, parent interviews, reviews of developmental histories, psychological testing, and assessments of speech and language.

Treatment

Two popular autism treatments are applied behavior analysis (ABA) and Floortime. Unconventional treatments include gluten- and casein-free diets and using chelation therapy to rid a child's body of toxic substances.

Research

Scientists are aggressively pursuing autism research, and studies have resulted in interesting findings about the brains of autistic people, as well as the role genetics and environment play in the development of autism.

Overview

"Autism, as I see it, steals the soul from a child; then, if allowed, relentlessly sucks life's marrow out of the family members, one by one."

—Jerry J. Kartzinel, *Louder than Words: A Mother's Journey in Healing Autism.*

"They see everything. They hear everything. They feel everything. But they can't tell anybody. They can't get it out."

—Michael Merzenich, quoted in Robert Bazell, "Autism Cases on the Rise Nationwide."

Autism is a highly complex disorder that affects the brain's ability to develop social and communication skills. It is one of five developmental disabilities known as autism spectrum disorders (ASDs), which include autistic disorder (usually just called autism), Asperger's syndrome, and two severe and rare forms of autism known as Rett syndrome and childhood disintegrative disorder. The fifth type of ASD is pervasive developmental disorder not otherwise specified (PDD-NOS), which is diagnosed when a child has autistic symptoms but does not necessarily meet all the criteria for autism. Because autism has so many different variations, it is not easily defined, as Robert Evert Cimera writes in his book, *Making Autism a Gift*: "Unfortunately, answering the question, 'What is autism?' is much like answering the question, 'What is life?' Certainly various people have their thoughts, theories, and opinions. Moreover, some people believe very firmly that only their view is completely correct. . . . You can't say that autism is any one thing in all cases."[1]

Children of all racial, ethnic, and social groups may be affected by autism, but it is about four times more common among boys than girls. Also, ASDs are often accompanied by other disorders. Nearly one-third of those diagnosed with autism, for instance, also have epilepsy, and many have at least some degree of mental retardation.

How Prevalent Is Autism?

The number of children diagnosed with autism appears to be rising at an unprecedented rate. During the early 1980s autism affected an estimated 4 or 5 children per 10,000 births. In February 2007 the Centers for Disease Control and Prevention (CDC) announced that the number had risen to one out of every 150 8-year-old children. Researchers cannot say whether this rise is due to an actual increase in cases of autism, changing criteria for diagnosing it, inconsistent survey techniques, or a combination of all three. Still, many scientists, health-care professionals, and autism advocacy organizations find the spike alarming. As National Institute of Mental Health (NIMH) director Thomas R. Insel explains: "I'm not convinced that this increase can be explained by differences in diagnosis. My own opinion is that there's been a very real increase in the last ten to fifteen years."[2]

> " Children of all racial, ethnic, and social groups may be affected by autism, but it is about four times more common among boys than girls. "

The Symptoms of Autism

Although no two autistic children exhibit exactly the same traits, there are commonalities. Symptoms range from mild to severe, depending on the intensity of the disorder. Some of the most common traits are not smiling by the age of 6 months; not babbling, pointing, or waving by 12 months; lack of interest in surroundings; avoidance of eye contact; and resistance to cuddling. As autistic toddlers get a little older, many exhibit self-stimulatory behaviors (called "stims") such as rocking back and forth, twirling in circles, or flapping their arms. They may be more interested in staring at a whirring ceiling fan than playing with toys. Many mimic words or phrases that are spoken to them (known as echolalia), hum or make unusual noises, and/or walk on their toes. Another typical autistic trait is meticulously lining up toys, cans from the cupboard, or other household objects on the floor or other surfaces. A woman named JC from Pleasant Grove, Utah, explains how she observed this in her autistic son: "His version of playing with his toys usually involved lining all his little army men or cars in perfect little lines on the table or stairs."[3] Some autistic children engage in self-abusive behavior such as biting or slapping themselves or banging their heads against a wall or the floor.

> Some autistic children engage in self-abusive behavior such as biting or slapping themselves or banging their heads against a wall or the floor.

Signs of autism are often evident in children who are 12 to 18 months old. But in about 25 percent of cases, symptoms do not show up until later, which is known as regressive autism. Children exhibit behavior characteristics and speech patterns that are normal and consistent with their age. Then they withdraw, avoid eye contact, and stop talking. This is what happened to Nicole Kalkowski's son, Ryan. When he was 14 months old, he was a bubbly, affectionate child who was willing to hug most anyone. He giggled a lot, blew kisses, loved to romp with his 2 older sisters, and was starting to put words together such as "hold you," "bye-bye," and "night-night." But just before Ryan's second birthday, his behavior abruptly changed. He stopped talking and rarely made eye contact with his family members. He refused to hug his sisters or play with them. When his mother tried to lift him out of his crib, he pushed her away. But the worst moment for Kalkowski was when she went into Ryan's room and found him on the floor, with his back to the door, rocking back and forth and lining up toy cars in a straight row. "At that moment, time stood still," she says. "I desperately called his name, but he wouldn't turn around. I wasn't asking one more person if something was wrong; I knew there was."[4]

Are Autistic Children Naturally Gifted?

Although some autistic children are musical prodigies or possess remarkable memorization or mathematical skills (known as autistic savants), the idea that this is true of all or even most children with autism is a myth. Eric Hollander, director of the Seaver and New York Autism Center of Excellence, explains:

> I think the public is really fascinated with these savant skills, as was demonstrated in the movie "Rain Man." It turns out that there are individuals with autism who have unbelievable skills, fantastic mathematical ability, certain abilities to learn languages, for example, outstanding visual-spatial abilities, or artistic abilities, or musical abilities, but that's really the exception rather than the rule.[5]

What Causes Autism?

Autism is a mysterious disorder. Scientists do not know exactly what causes it, although studies have shown that it is linked to abnormal chemistry in the brain; that is, autistic people's brains are "wired" differently than those of nonautistic people. As journalist Claudia Wallis states:

> Once thought to be mainly a disease of the cerebellum—a region in the back of the brain that integrates sensory and motor activity, autism is increasingly seen as a pervasive problem with the way the brain is wired. The distribution of white matter, the nerve fibers that link diverse parts of the brain, is abnormal, but it's not clear how much is the cause and how much the result of autism.[6]

According to Insel, research with identical twins has shown that if one child has autism, the other has a 60 to 91 percent chance of being affected by it. From this scientists infer a strong likelihood that autism has genetic roots. Genetic vulnerabilities could then be triggered by various external or environmental factors. Even though no specific genes have been identified as causing autism, researchers are optimistic that further genetic studies will pave the way toward a better understanding of potential causes.

Researchers have also made other discoveries about ASDs. They tend to occur more often among children who have accompanying medical conditions such as fragile X syndrome, which is a form of mental retardation; tuberous sclerosis, a rare genetic disorder that causes benign tumors to grow in the brain and other vital organs; and congenital rubella, physical ailments that are passed to an infant when his or her mother is infected with the virus that causes German measles. The CDC also says that some harmful drugs taken during pregnancy, such as the prescription drug thalidomide, have been linked with a higher risk of autism in children.

Do Vaccinations Cause Autism?

The potential connection between autism and childhood vaccinations is a topic of major controversy. Many parents say that their children were perfectly normal until they got vaccinated; soon afterward, their health and behavior radically changed. Thus far, parents have blamed vaccinations for nearly 5,000 cases of autism. One of the most famous involves Hannah Poling, who was a happy, affectionate toddler who babbled constantly, waved at her father when he left for work, and was speaking a number of words by the time she was 19 months old. Because Hannah had suffered from a series of ear infections, she had fallen behind in getting her vaccines. In July 2000 her mother took her to the doctor, who gave Hannah 9 inoculations—an unusually high amount for one visit. Several days later, Hannah developed a fever, cried and screamed, stopped eating, and would no longer walk. Over the following months her condition continued to worsen, and in 2001 she was diagnosed as autistic. Hannah's parents learned that many of the vaccines their daughter had received contained thimerosal, a vaccine preservative that is nearly 50 percent mercury. Because mercury is highly toxic, and the onset of Hannah's autism occurred short-

> **Although some autistic children are musical prodigies or possess remarkable memorization or mathematical skills (known as autistic savants), the idea that this is true of all or even most children with autism is a myth.**

A speech pathologist works with Hannah, 3, who has been diagnosed with autism. Autism affects the brain's normal development of social and communication skills.

ly after her vaccinations, the Polings were convinced that the shots were to blame. In a landmark case during 2007, the federal government conceded that vaccines could possibly have hurt Hannah and agreed to compensate the Polings for her care.

Since 2001 thimerosal has no longer been used in most regular vaccinations for children six years of age or younger. But the Food and Drug Administration (FDA) says that the removal of thimerosal was merely a precautionary measure. The agency maintains that the preservative is safe and that its association with autism or other childhood disorders is speculative rather than factual. Those who disagree argue that thimerosal's mercury content makes it toxic, especially to young children whose brains have not yet fully developed.

How Autism Is Diagnosed

The diagnosis of autism starts with parents: If they observe that their child is not developing normally or is exhibiting stims or other unusual behaviors, it is important that they seek professional help as soon as possible. Trisha Macnair explains: "Sometimes parents just have a strong instinct something isn't quite right with their child and this feeling should never be ignored."[7] Unfortunately, there is no medical test that can diagnose autism. Health-care professionals perform a comprehensive evaluation that typically includes clinical observations, parent interviews, reviews of developmental histories, psychological testing, and assessments of speech and language. If autism is suspected, clinicians use a variety of screening tools to make a final diagnosis. This is often done by a multidisciplinary team of health-care professionals, including pediatricians, child psychiatrists, physical therapists, speech/language therapists, and social workers.

About half of all autistic children are not diagnosed before kindergarten, often because parents do not recognize the warning signs. When actress Jenny McCarthy's son, Evan, was a toddler, he seemed distant and did not want to cuddle very much. He flapped his arms and walked in circles, was mesmerized by spinning the wheels on his toy trucks, and seemed most entertained by fiddling with door hinges or lining up his toys in straight lines. Still, McCarthy did not see these as autism symptoms because, as with many parents, she did not know what to look for. Then when Evan was two years old, he began having life-threatening seizures. After a series of physical exams and behavioral evaluations, a pediatric neurologist told McCarthy that Evan was autistic, and she was completely stunned, as she explains: "I felt each membrane and vein in my heart shattering into a million pieces. Nothing prepared me for this. I couldn't breathe. I wanted it gone. I had been through so much with seizures and psychotic reactions to meds. I looked

> " About half of all autistic children are not diagnosed before kindergarten, often because parents do not recognize the warning signs. "

This autistic student is tutored at the West Virginia Autistic Training Center in Huntington, West Virginia. Autism is about four times more common among boys than girls.

at the doctor with pleading, tearful eyes, 'This can't be. He is very loving and sweet and not anything like 'Rain Man.'"[8] McCarthy learned that not all autistic children display the same symptoms. Even though a child may be loving and affectionate, there are other warning signs that parents just do not recognize.

How Autism Is Treated

Specific autism treatment programs may vary widely, depending on the severity of the disorder and the child's individual needs. As Margaret Strock of the NIMH writes:

> An effective treatment program will build on the child's interests, offer a predictable schedule, teach tasks as a series of simple steps, actively engage the child's attention in highly structured activities, and provide regular reinforcement of behavior. . . . Recognizing that parents are the child's earliest teachers, more programs are beginning to train parents to continue the therapy at home.[9]

One of the most common autism treatments is known as applied behavior analysis (ABA), an intensive, 40- to 50-hour-per-week home-based education program. Another is Floortime, which was developed by child psychiatrist Stanley Greenspan and involves parents or therapists getting on the floor and engaging the child in play-based activities. The goal of Floortime is to help autistic children become good thinkers, develop social skills, understand their own emotions, and build relationships.

How Effective Are Autism Treatments?

Although no one treatment works equally well for all autistic children, a number of treatment programs have proved to be very effective. The success of these treatments often varies from child to child, depending on how severe the disorder is. Also, studies have consistently shown that the earlier autism is diagnosed and treated, the more successful the treatment will be. Joanne and Tom Palmer's son, Carson, started exhibiting autistic symptoms at about 18 months of age. He had severe tantrums, would not let anyone touch him, and seemed to be getting more and more out of control. After he was diagnosed with autism, the Palmers enrolled him in an intensive early intervention preschool especially for children with ASD. Through the specialized therapy and instruction he received, Carson began to thrive; and not only did his temper tantrums stop, but he started communicating with his parents. "Now," says Joanne Palmer, "instead of worrying about what's going to happen, we're totally confident that Carson's going to have a normal future. . . . Now we have our child back; we can do anything and go anywhere."[10]

Some people have opted to use treatments for autism that many health-care professionals denounce, saying that no scientific proof exists that they are effective. One of the most controversial therapies is chelation (kee-LAY-shun), a detoxification treatment that was developed by the U.S. Navy in the 1940s to treat lead poisoning. When chelation is used in autism treatment, it is based on the theory that heavy metals such as mercury contribute to autism. By purging the body of these metals, proponents say, autism symptoms can diminish and even disappear. The late Bernard Rimland, a psychologist and the father of an autistic man, was an outspoken advocate of chelation treatments, as he stated in 2002: "There is no question that chelation, taking the mercury out of the kids, is by far the most effective treatment available."[11]

> The success of [autism] treatments often varies from child to child, depending on how severe the disorder is.

Autism Success Stories

The more researchers learn about autism, the brighter the prognosis is for children who have it, especially for those who are diagnosed early while their brains are still developing. Over time some autistic children respond so well to treatment that they no longer need specialized education programs and are placed in mainstream classes at school. Campion Quinn, the father of an autistic boy, says that some children with autism who receive the right treatment and social support grow up to lead lives that are normal or nearly normal.

One example of someone who overcame the hurdles of autism and succeeded in life is Temple Grandin. She did not talk until she was 3½ years old, and in 1950 she was diagnosed with autism. Her parents were told that there was no hope for her, and they were advised to institutionalize her. Yet today Grandin holds a PhD and is one of the most respected livestock equipment designers in the world. She often speaks publicly about the stigma of autism and what it means for those who have it. She writes:

I have read enough to know that there are still many parents, and, yes, professionals, too, who believe that "once autistic, always autistic." This dictum has meant sad and sorry lives for many children diagnosed, as I was in early life, as autistic. To these people, it is incomprehensible that the characteristics of autism can be modified and controlled. However, I feel strongly that I am living proof that they can.[12]

Another autism success story is Jason McElwain, a young man from Rochester, New York. When he was a toddler, he exhibited all the classic signs of autism, such as no eye contact, not wanting to be hugged, head banging, hypersensitivity, refusal to eat, and angry outbursts, and he was diagnosed as severely autistic. At the age of 5 he still did not talk, and his parents did not know if he would ever get better. Then about a year later he began to break through the autism and responded well to his specialized classes at school. By the time he was at Greece Athena High School, he had become the manager of the basketball team. Although he had never played in a game, on February 15, 2006, with 4 minutes left on the clock, his coach decided to give him a chance. Jason walked out on the court determined to make a basket—and by the time the game was over, "J-Mac" had scored 20 points, including 6 3-pointers, and was riding on the shoulders of his teammates, who were calling him a hero.

Will New Research Prevent or Cure Autism?

As research continues to progress, scientists may someday unlock the mysteries of autism and find the cure that they seek. New studies are revealing interesting findings about the brains of autistic people, as well as the role genetics and environment plays in the development of autism. Yet not everyone is enthusiastic about autism research. Some autistic people are resentful of it, saying that autism makes them unique and they have no interest in being cured. That is the perspective of James Medhurst, an autistic man from the United Kingdom, who writes:

We are often accused of being in denial. Surely, we are asked, if someone could wave a magic wand and all physical or mental quirks could be excised, anyone would be foolish not to take the opportunity. It is true that there are certainly days when I feel like that, but these are my bad days, when I would not regard myself as making my best decisions. . . . But if there really was a magic wand, I know what I would do. I would cure myself for one day, just to see what it was like to be normal, knowing that I could use the same magic wand to return myself to the real me afterwards.[13]

What Is Autism?

❝Autism is what every parent of an autistic child says it is. It also is what doctors and scientists say it is. . . . There are contradictions and controversies and perhaps, above all else, moving and emotional stories to be told about autism and its impact on individuals and the people who love them.❞

—Tim Langmaid, "Autism & CNN."

❝Often they are not out of tune with this world but, ironically, far too aware of it. The world is too much with them, and because they are excruciatingly sensitive, they're forced to retreat.❞

—Patricia Stacey, "Floor Time."

When Julie Kosloski was in high school, she volunteered at a residential facility in Evergreen, Colorado, that was home to young people with a wide variety of physical and mental issues. Those with autism were severely autistic, and because she had never had experience with the disorder before, the children captured her attention. She explains:

> I was naturally drawn to them. It was as though they were locked in their own worlds, completely oblivious to danger, or evil, or the importance of behaving appropriately, or even wearing clothes. I often found myself wondering, "Is our world really better than theirs?" I longed to find

the magic key that would somehow unlock the door to their world so I could reach them.[14]

Kosloski was so captivated by the autistic children that when she turned 18, she took a permanent position at the facility. After graduating from college, she became a teacher of emotionally impaired children in Denver.

Autism Spectrum Disorders

The word *autism* originates from the Greek word *autos* meaning "self." It was first introduced in 1911 by Swiss psychiatrist Eugen Bleuler, who used autism to describe adult schizophrenic patients who were socially withdrawn and kept to themselves. In 1943 child psychiatrist Leo Kanner of Johns Hopkins Hospital published a paper in which he used the term *early infantile autism* to describe a group of developmentally impaired children he had studied for several years. Kanner observed that the children displayed symptoms such as aloofness and absence of eye contact, could not communicate effectively, and were strongly resistant to changes in their routines. They also exhibited peculiar behaviors such as repetition of meaningless words, rocking back and forth, making odd sounds, and flapping their hands. In 1944, unaware of Kanner's work, an Austrian pediatrician named Hans Asperger published a paper about a similar autistic disorder, one whose symptoms were not as severe as those of autism. Asperger's writing was based on observations of young boys who had normal intelligence and language development, but who were highly self-absorbed, lacked empathy, and were deficient in social and communication skills. These milder symptoms are typical of the ASD that came to be known as Asperger's syndrome.

> " In the past autism was considered an extremely rare disorder that only affected 4 or 5 children per 10,000. "

In the past autism was considered an extremely rare disorder that only affected 4 or 5 children per 10,000. Over time, however, the number has steadily risen to 1 in 150 children, as reported by the CDC in February 2007. One possible reason for the marked increase in autism cases is the range of developmental disorders that are included in the group of ASDs, which were introduced in 1970 by Lorna Wing, a British psychiatrist and the mother of an autistic child, and her colleague Judith Gould. Barbara Firestone, author of the book *Autism Heroes*, explains: "They characterized autism as a range of disorders based on difficulties with social interaction, communication and imagination. It encompasses children whose symptoms vary in type and intensity."[15]

Severe Autism

The impairments associated with autism can vary widely depending on the intensity of the disorder. Children who are severely autistic tend to have serious communication difficulties, with an estimated 50 percent lacking the ability to talk. They also have problems interacting with others, shy away from eye contact, and engage in self-abusive behavior. Rita Rubin, whose daughter Sue was diagnosed with severe autism at the age of four, explains what it was like to witness this:

> She did a lot of self-abusive behavior. She did a lot of biting of her own hand and arm and she was a head-banger. We had to watch her every single minute. If you weren't watching her it meant she was doing something awful. Something that would break the plumbing or cause a fire or do something dangerous. So there was always tension and it was just moving from one difficult situation to another, from one crisis to another. As a parent it is the most painful thing you can imagine, to see your child hitting herself and throwing her head against the car window or throwing her head against the table or on a concrete floor. It is horrible to have to watch your own child hurt herself that way.[16]

Severely autistic children also frequently engage in repetitive behaviors. Kosloski remembers this trait in an autistic boy she worked with at the Colorado residential facility. "Unlike many kids with autism, 'Marcus' was sweet and affectionate, and often climbed up on my lap," she says. "But he spent whole days just walking back and forth, back and forth, between two trees, while flapping his hands and making these peculiar sounds. That was his routine and he did not want it disrupted." She recalls an autistic girl at the facility whose behavior was very different:

> She was like a wild little thing who screamed whenever one of us tried to touch her. We couldn't hang curtains in her bedroom because she'd rip them right off the rods, and once she threw a chair across the room and it went crashing through the window. Then there was the time when we were outside, and I noticed that she was closely watching another student who was in a wheelchair. All of a sudden she jumped up, darted across the lawn, disengaged the brake, and shoved the wheelchair down the hill, and we all had to chase after it. It was heading straight toward Marcus as he was doing his usual tree walking, and it scared him so badly that he started jumping up and down in place, flapping his hands wildly and making loud "AACK! AACK! AACK!" noises. That was quite a day![17]

> **" One reason severely autistic children become easily agitated or frightened is because they are often hypersensitive to light, noise, and motion. "**

One reason severely autistic children become easily agitated or frightened is because they are often hypersensitive to light, noise, and motion. According to a report by the NIMH, many children with autism have faulty sensory mechanisms, which can jar them, causing them to be easily confused and scared. Patricia Stacey, whose son is autistic, describes this:

> Imagine your sensory world scrambled and unregulated, your auditory intake a rock station—or worse, mere static—blasting incessantly in your ears. Imagine your kitchen light as bright as a searchlight, boring into your cornea every time you turn it on. Imagine yourself in clothes so irritating that they seem lined with metal scraping brushes.

Imagine entering a restaurant and encountering fumes so overpowering to your eyes that you think the cook must be boiling Mace. This can be the world of the autistic.[18]

"He Can't Put on a Social Front"

Milder forms of autism, including Asperger's syndrome, are not always easy to identify in children. Children with milder autism may have normal to above-average intelligence but poor social skills and make little or no eye contact, which can make them seem obstinate or uncooperative toward others. But the reality is, they often lack an understanding of how they are supposed to behave, or wonder why they must conform to other people's expectations when they do not seem to make sense. Alan Hope, a journalist who lives in Belgium, has a son with Asperger's syndrome. He describes some of the challenges the boy encounters in school:

> He has the usual social problems. . . . He can't put on a social front and just ignores people he isn't comfortable with. He runs into problems in school when the teacher gives an instruction, which he takes literally when it wasn't meant so. He doesn't get sarcasm, for instance. If he yawns, and the teacher says, "Hey, why don't you go lie down and get some sleep," he'll consider that to be an instruction, not a wisecrack.[19]

Hope adds that his son needs to have things explained to him literally because he cannot understand clichés or indirect instructions. He explains:

> It's no use telling him, "Now do a drawing of what you saw today on our trip." You need to tell him, "Get your pencils out, take some paper, sit at a free desk" . . . and so on. While other kids in the class react instinctively to fill in the gaps, he can't function without explicit instructions. If you said, say, "Sit down and draw a picture," he'd sit down and then be distraught because he can't draw without his pencils, which are on the other side of the room.[20]

Parents of children with Asperger's syndrome or other higher-

functioning types of autism sometimes become frustrated over
their children's unwillingness to
cuddle, engage in conversations,
or play games. They may misin-
terpret these behaviors and assume
that the children are not happy
or do not love them. Teddi Cole,
whose daughter Mary has higher-
functioning autism, offers her own
personal example of this:

> **Sometimes, though, parents find the idea of having an autistic child too painful to bear, so they ignore the symptoms and hope that they will eventually disappear.**

I remember sitting in
Mary's room one day and
trying to get her to engage
with me in playing a game. And she didn't engage, she
didn't want to engage, and I started to cry. . . . She turned
around and said, "Mommy, you want a Popsicle?" which
was a treat I'd offer her if she were upset. While I ate
my Popsicle, I looked at her and watched her playing
and I thought, "You know what? This kid is happy. She's
okay. I'm the one that's unhappy." In that moment I real-
ized that I needed to change the way I looked at her, I
needed to meet her halfway. I needed to find out how she
thought and how she viewed life, as opposed to trying to
get her to completely see how we did things, trying to get
her to do things our way. That moment freed me.[21]

Deeply Hidden Capabilities

Because many autistic people cannot talk, they are often thought to be
severely mentally retarded and unable to learn. This assumption, however, has proved to be erroneous in more than one instance. A young girl
from New York named Hannah was diagnosed as severely autistic when
she was a child. Even after years of intensive therapy, when she was 13
much of her speech was unintelligible, and her way of speaking was often
limited to tidbits of songs or words spoken by others that she merely
echoed. Doctors told her parents that she was likely retarded and would

never be able to read or write. But in October 2004 Hannah proved them wrong. She was given a specialized computer keyboard, and when one of her therapists asked if there was anything she wanted to say, with her mother watching, she typed "I love Mom." Hannah, who was once thought to be incapable of learning, showed that she had an extensive vocabulary, a sense of humor, and a natural talent for mathematics. In May 2006 her tutor, Tonette Jacob, presented her with a page of about 30 math problems. After one quick glimpse, Hannah astonished Jacob by typing all 30 answers. Jacob asked the girl if she had a photographic memory, and Hannah typed "Yes."[22]

> "Some autistic children may never learn to talk, socialize, or live independently, while others have managed to break through their barriers and now live happy, fulfilling lives.

Sue Rubin, a young woman from Whittier, California, is another living example of how very misunderstood an autistic person can be. Rubin could not talk and was believed to be severely retarded, with a mental capacity of a 2½-year-old. Just before her thirteenth birthday, she was given a keyboard so that she could learn to communicate. That, she says, is when her "mind began to wake up." She explains the frustration she and many other autistic people share: "Autism is a world so difficult to explain to someone who is not autistic, someone who can easily turn off the peculiar movements and actions that take over our bodies."[23] Once she learned to type, Rubin's intelligence became obvious to everyone around her. By the time she was in her twenties, she was attending college and had written the narration for an Oscar-nominated documentary called *Autism Is a World*.

When Parents Are in Denial

It is never easy for people to hear that their child is autistic, and often it is a devastating blow. Many parents react to the news by denying that it is true, at least initially. Perhaps their child lines up toys, or hums a lot, or flaps his or her arms, but they may dismiss these symptoms as merely quirky behaviors. If a child does not respond when spoken to, parents may assume that he or she has a hearing problem, or is just being stubborn.

Sometimes, though, parents find the idea of having an autistic child too painful to bear, so they ignore the symptoms and hope that they will eventually disappear. Kosloski encountered this with a child at the school where she was a special needs teacher. He was in a regular kindergarten class, and the teacher grew exasperated with his behavior and asked Kosloski to take a look at him. She explains what she observed:

> I've seen enough autistic kids to know right away that this boy had autism. The symptoms were so obvious—he wouldn't make eye contact, he made humming noises all the time, he wouldn't let you touch him, he rocked back and forth in his chair, he blurted things that had nothing to do with what was going on. He would not play, had no friends, and spent his recess time walking around the playground all by himself. My heart just went out to him. I checked into what services were available and set up a meeting with his parents, but they said no, absolutely not, our son is not autistic. They were in total denial. As far as I know he never got tested or received any therapy that could have helped him, and it still really bothers me.[24]

Lingering Questions

Much has been learned about autism since it was first identified in the 1900s. Yet it remains mysterious, a disorder that scientists and health-care professionals still do not fully understand. Some autistic children may never learn to talk, socialize, or live independently, while others have managed to break through their barriers and now live happy, fulfilling lives. No one can say what the future holds. But with autism cases continuing to increase as rapidly as they are, researchers' efforts to unlock the secrets of this baffling developmental disorder will likely intensify in the years to come.

What Is Autism?

❝ Based on statistics from the U.S. Department of Education and other governmental agencies, autism is growing at a startling rate of 10–17 percent per year. At this rate, the ASA estimates that the prevalence of autism could reach 4 million Americans in the next decade. ❞

—Autism Society of America, "What Are Autism Spectrum Disorders?" January 23, 2008. www.autism-society.org.

The Autism Society of America (ASA), which was founded in 1965 by parents of children with autism, seeks to improve the lives of everyone affected by autism spectrum disorders.

❝ The explosive increase [in autism] that has been claimed is almost certainly not true. The numbers, if they're rising, are not rising very quickly, if . . . at all. ❞

—Stephen Goodman, "Diagnosis: Autism," *60 Minutes*, CBS News, February 18, 2007.

Goodman is an epidemiologist at Johns Hopkins University who has reviewed autism statistics for the past 30 years.

Bracketed quotes indicate conflicting positions.

* Editor's Note: While the definition of a primary source can be narrowly or broadly defined, for the purposes of Compact Research, a primary source consists of: 1) results of original research presented by an organization or researcher; 2) eyewitness accounts of events, personal experience, or work experience; 3) first-person editorials offering pundits' opinions; 4) government officials presenting political plans and/or policies; 5) representatives of organizations presenting testimony or policy.

66 Autism's sinister attack on children that start out appearing healthy, even precocious, is one of the most devastating trials a parent can endure. **99**

—Monya De, "What Causes Autism?" *The World Newser*, ABC News, June 18, 2007. http://blogs.abcnews.com.

De is with the ABC News Medical Unit.

66 Everybody talks so negatively about autism, almost as if it were cancer or a death sentence or something horrible from the Dark Ages. Autism isn't horrible. It isn't a death sentence. People with autism aren't destined to be failures. . . . They're merely people who are, in some ways, different than the 'typical' person. **99**

—Robert Evert Cimera, *Making Autism a Gift*. Lanham, MD: Rowman & Littlefield, 2007.

Cimera has a PhD in special education and has taught autistic students at all grade levels, including college.

66 Even if you account for over-diagnoses and other factors, the increase and current rate is terrifying. **99**

—Rock Positano, "Autism Spectrum Disorders a Focus of HBO Special," *Huffington Post*, March 28, 2008. www.huffingtonpost.com.

Positano is a physician from New York City.

66 The frequency of the diagnosis has clearly increased but that doesn't tell you beans. **99**

—William Barbaresi, quoted in Jacqueline Stenson, "As Autism Cases Soar, a Search for Clues," *Health*, MSNBC, February 24, 2005. www.msnbc.msn.com.

Barbaresi is a pediatrician at the Mayo Clinic in Rochester, Minnesota.

> **66** Sometimes my mind feels noisy, but I'd never wish for my autism to go away. It helps me focus. **99**

—Delaney Rodgers, quoted in Joanne Fowler, "'Would I Trade in My Autism? No,'" *People Weekly*, May 8, 2006.

Rodgers is a young woman who was diagnosed with Asperger's syndrome when she was eight years old.

> **66** I don't like my autism because I get anxious. It makes my stomach hurt. . . . Sounds bother me. At the movies, when it's so loud, I sometimes cry and have to cover my ears. **99**

—Andrew Gering, quoted in Joanne Fowler, "'Would I Trade in My Autism? No,'" *People Weekly*, May 8, 2006.

Gering is an autistic teenage boy.

> **66** I looked at Evan and saw him flapping and once again had my heart shattered. I had always looked at it like an adorable Evan characteristic, so cute and unique that I even called him my little bird. . . . Everything I thought was cute was a sign of autism and I felt tricked. **99**

—Jenny McCarthy, "The Day I Heard My Son Had Autism," CNN.com, September 24, 2007. www.cnn.com.

McCarthy is an actress whose son, Evan, is autistic.

> **66** If I were talking to a parent of an autistic child who had just gotten the diagnosis, I would want them to know that they will find their place, and that they will find peace with it—in their own way. **99**

—Suzanne Reyes, quoted in Barbara Firestone, *Autism Heroes*. London and Philadelphia: Jessica Kingsley, 2008.

Reyes's daughter, Calida, was diagnosed with an autism spectrum disorder at the age of 20 months.

---

66 People with autism ... have difficulty interpreting non-verbal cues, such as gestures and facial expressions or putting themselves inside someone else's head or drawing understanding from anything other than the literal meaning of words. 99

—Malcolm Gladwell, *Blink: The Power of Thinking Without Thinking*. New York: Little, Brown.

Gladwell is a staff writer with the *New Yorker* magazine and the author of two books.

66 He started showing signs of temper and violent urges towards his mother and sister. It was as if he couldn't control his frustration: his mind wanted to do or say one thing, but he couldn't follow through. 99

—Alan Hope, interview with author, April 29, 2008.

Hope, who is a journalist living in Belgium, has a son with Asperger's syndrome.

Facts and Illustrations

What Is Autism?

- Since the 1970s autism cases have risen from 4 or 5 per 10,000 children to **1 in 150**.

- An estimated **1 million to 1.5 million** people in the United States have autism.

- Approximately **50 percent** of autistic children cannot talk.

- Autism is about **4 times more common** in boys than girls.

- Approximately **1 in 94 boys** has some sort of autism spectrum disorder.

- More than **60 children** are diagnosed with autism each day.

- According to Autism Speaks, more children are diagnosed with **autism each year than AIDS, diabetes, and cancer combined**.

- A 2006 study by the Harvard School of Public Health showed that it can cost more than **$3 million** to care for an autistic person over his or her lifetime. The same study showed that caring for all autistic people over their lifetimes costs an estimated **$35 billion** per year.

- The Individuals with Disabilities Act guarantees that children with autism are entitled to a **free public education** that is appropriate for their needs.

- The United States Office of Special Education Programs says that the majority of children with disabilities (including autism) are being educated at their **neighborhood schools** along with nondisabled students.

Autism Cases on the Rise

The number of children diagnosed with autism has risen from 4 or 5 per 10,000 in the 1970s to 1 per 150 children today—and according to the advocacy group Fighting Autism, a new case of autism is diagnosed every 21 minutes. This graph shows that since 1992, autism cases have spiked more than 1,300 percent.

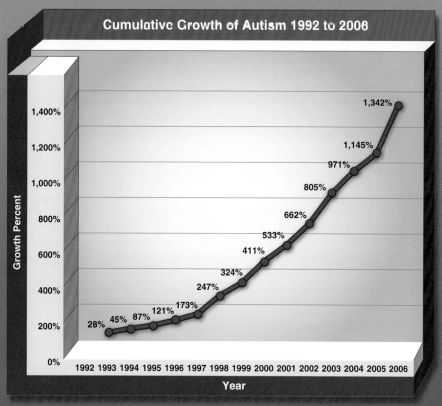

Cumulative Growth of Autism 1992 to 2006

Source: "Number of Cases Cumulative Growth," Fighting Autism, 2007. www.fightingautism.org.

Signs of Autism

While no two autistic children necessarily display the same behavioral traits and symptoms, there are a number of commonalities. Symptoms can vary widely based on the severity of the disorder. This chart shows some of the most typical traits exhibited by autistic children.

- Lack of interest in "pretend" games such as pretending to feed a doll
- Not pointing at objects to show interest, such as an airplane flying over
- Not looking when another person points at an object
- Trouble relating to others, avoidance of eye contact, unresponsive when spoken to (but aware of other sounds)
- Lack of desire to cuddle or show affection
- Lack of empathy: problems understanding other people's feelings
- Prefers being alone rather than playing with other children
- Repeats or echoes words or phrases in place of normal language (echolalia)
- Trouble expressing needs using typical words or motions
- Needs consistency: problems adapting when routine changes
- Hypersensitive to sounds, light, motion; unusual reactions to the way things smell, taste, look, feel, or sound
- Peculiar repetitive motions such as hand flapping or toe walking
- Frustration over lack of ability to communicate may lead to temper tantrums, or even self-abusive behavior or abuse toward others

Source: Melody Stevens et al., "Prevalence of the Autism Spectrum Disorders (ASDs) in Multiple Areas of the United States, 2000 and 2002," Autism Developmental Disabilities Monitoring Network, 2007.

- The number of children receiving special school services for autism rose from 22,445 in 1995 to 140,254 in 2004, a **525 percent** increase.

Autism Prevalence by State

According to the CDC, the estimated prevalence of autism in the United States is one in every 150 children. As this graph shows, some states have a much higher rate, while in others the rate is much lower.

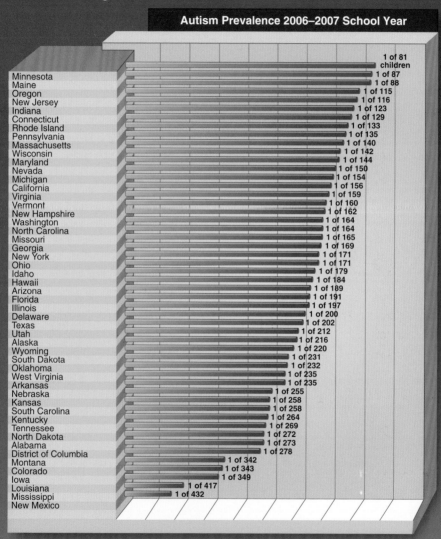

Autism Prevalence 2006–2007 School Year

State	Prevalence
	1 of 81 children
Minnesota	1 of 87
Maine	1 of 88
Oregon	1 of 115
New Jersey	1 of 116
Indiana	1 of 123
Connecticut	1 of 129
Rhode Island	1 of 133
Pennsylvania	1 of 135
Massachusetts	1 of 140
Wisconsin	1 of 142
Maryland	1 of 144
Nevada	1 of 150
Michigan	1 of 154
California	1 of 156
Virginia	1 of 159
Vermont	1 of 160
New Hampshire	1 of 162
Washington	1 of 164
North Carolina	1 of 164
Missouri	1 of 165
Georgia	1 of 169
New York	1 of 171
Ohio	1 of 171
Idaho	1 of 179
Hawaii	1 of 184
Arizona	1 of 189
Florida	1 of 191
Illinois	1 of 197
Delaware	1 of 200
Texas	1 of 202
Utah	1 of 212
Alaska	1 of 216
Wyoming	1 of 220
South Dakota	1 of 231
Oklahoma	1 of 232
West Virginia	1 of 235
Arkansas	1 of 235
Nebraska	1 of 255
Kansas	1 of 258
South Carolina	1 of 258
Kentucky	1 of 264
Tennessee	1 of 269
North Dakota	1 of 272
Alabama	1 of 273
District of Columbia	1 of 278
Montana	1 of 342
Colorado	1 of 343
Iowa	1 of 349
Louisiana	1 of 417
Mississippi	1 of 432
New Mexico	

Note: Statistics are based on public school enrollment and do not include students that attend private schools, are home schooled, or are in regular education classes. States have different eligibility criteria for the autism disability category, which may influence the prevalence numbers that are reported.

Source: "Autism Prevalence, Public Schools State Rankings," Fighting Autism, 2007. wwwfightingautism.org.

Reasons Doctors Do Not Screen for Autism

Health-care experts repeatedly state that the earlier autism spectrum disorders are diagnosed and treated, the better the child's chances will be to make significant improvement. Parents may not notice symptoms in a baby but if pediatricians screen for autism during well-baby visits, the disorder could possibly be caught early. Studies have shown, however, that this does not happen often enough. A survey published in April 2006 showed that 82 percent of pediatricians performed routine developmental screening, but only 8 percent performed screening for Autism Spectrum Disorders. This graph indicates the reasons they gave for not screening for autism. Some doctors chose more than one reason.

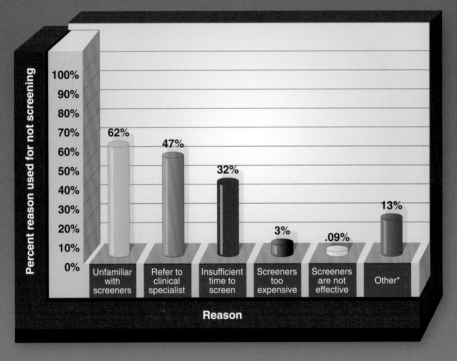

*Other reasons include use of clinical judgment, resource constraints, not necessary, or not applicable to their practice.

Source: Susan Dosreis et al., "Autism Spectrum Disorder Screening and Management Practices Among General Pediatric Providers," *Developmental and Behavioral Pediatrics*, April 2006, pp. 88–94.

What Causes Autism?

> **Is it cellphones? Ultrasound? Diet sodas? Every parent has a theory. At this point, we just don't know.**
>
> —Tom Insel, quoted in Gardiner Harris and Anahad O'Connor, "On Autism's Cause, It's Parents vs. Research."

> **Autistic individuals may not be 'different' from the rest of us but simply 'more sensitive' to environmental injury—they may be the 'canaries in the coal mine' warning us of impending greater disaster.**
>
> —Martha R. Herbert, "Time to Get a Grip."

After introducing the term *early infantile autism* in 1943, Leo Kanner went on to opine about probable causes. He concluded that the developmental disorder was likely brought on by parents who were unaffectionate and lacked warmth, whom he described as "just happening to defrost enough to produce a child."[25] In a paper published in 1949, Kanner elaborated further, saying that autistic children were the result of cold, distant mothers. This "refrigerator mother" theory, as it came to be known, was widely embraced by medical professionals. It was perpetuated during the 1950s and 1960s in a number of writings by the influential Austrian psychotherapist Bruno Bettelheim—and as erroneous as the belief was, it was rarely challenged. As a result, mothers who were told that their child was autistic suffered not only grief, but also crushing guilt, blame, and self-doubt.

Numerous theories exist about what causes autism, but scientists are the first to admit that they are only theories. Some studies have shown that older fathers have a higher risk of having autistic children, while others point to a possible link between autism and ultrasound during pregnancy. As varied as all the theories are, it is widely believed that autism is caused by a combination of factors, as the National Institutes of Health (NIH) explains: "Because the disorder is so complex, and because no two people with autism are exactly alike, autism is probably the result of many causes."[26] Many scientists are convinced that autism has genetic roots. According to the NIH, 10 or more genes on different chromosomes could potentially play a role in autism. Some of those genes may place a person at greater risk for developing the disorder, while others may cause particular symptoms or determine the severity of the symptoms.

Scientists are aggressively pursuing genetic research because autism is one of the most hereditary disorders. Research shows that if one identical twin is autistic, the other has a 60 to 91 percent chance of also having autism. Pinpointing a particular gene or genes has long proved to be a daunting task. But in October 2006 researchers at the Vanderbilt Kennedy Center for Research on Human Development announced that they had made progress toward solving the puzzle. The team, led by Pat Levitt and Daniel Campbell, identified a genetic variant associated with the MET gene (typically connected with cancer) that more than doubled the risk of a child developing autism. This was considered a breakthrough finding because MET affects not only the brain and nervous system, but also plays a role in repairing the immune system and intestines. Levitt says the discovery is especially intriguing because autistic children typically suffer from digestive and immune system problems. His team also discovered that the activity of the gene was affected by what is known as oxidative stress, which is damage that can be caused by excessive exposure to toxins. Levitt explains: "Genes create a vulnerability that then gets coupled with some environmental disturbance—but right now, we don't have any idea what those factors might be."[27] This research could pave the way toward

> " Scientists are aggressively pursuing genetic research because autism is one of the most hereditary disorders. "

more discoveries about the role genetics, combined with other factors, play in the development of autism.

What Role Does the Environment Play?

In recent years, researchers have begun looking more closely at the link between autism and environmental degradation. According to Martha R. Herbert it is not enough to assume that autism is purely a disorder of the brain. Rather, it must be viewed as a disorder of the whole body that *affects* the brain, meaning that environmental factors serve as possible triggers. She explains: "Observations about environmental factors relevant to autism go back decades, though they have been obscured in recent years by the dominance of a genetic focus. . . . In addition, a claim that autism is predominantly genetic rests on an assumption that our environment is stable and/or that we are not affected by environmental changes."[28]

Herbert notes that during the same period of time in which autism cases have skyrocketed, significant damage has been inflicted on the environment. Toxic chemicals such as pesticides and industrial solvents are being used today more than ever before, and this has led to air, water, and land becoming increasingly more polluted. "Given this pervasive environmental instability," she writes, "we must ask ourselves, 'Why would human children, and their developing brain and bodily systems, be spared?' In fact, given their delicacy, there is every reason to expect that children and their developing brains and bodies will be particularly affected."[29]

To explore the environment's link to autism in greater depth, scientists have conducted studies in certain areas where the number of autistic children is unusually high. In April 2008 researchers from the University of Texas Health Science Center at San Antonio announced the results

> " Even though these findings do not necessarily prove that autism is caused or exacerbated by pollution, the researchers say that this is definitely a red flag and the connection should be explored in greater depth. "

of such a study. For the first time, the researchers showed a significant link between industrial toxins in the environment and increased rates of autism. Also significant was that the largest increase in rates of autism occurred in counties that had the highest amount of industrial waste discharge—in other words, the closer families lived to the pollution, the higher the incidence of autism. Even though these findings do not necessarily prove that autism is caused or exacerbated by pollution, the researchers say that this is definitely a red flag and the connection should be explored in greater depth.

Is Autism Caused by Mercury Poisoning?

The possible connection between mercury and autism is a source of intense interest for many scientists. Medical writer Daniel J. DeNoon describes its toxicity: "Mercury is one heck of a toxic substance. A fraction of a teaspoon can render all the fish in a 20-acre lake unsafe to eat."[30] Mercury occurs naturally in the environment but is also emitted by coal-fired power plants and other industrial sources. Once it is airborne it may travel for miles before it is deposited onto soil or in water, where chemical reactions or natural bacteria convert it to the most toxic form of mercury, known as methylmercury. In waterways it works its way up the aquatic food chain and continues to accumulate at progressively higher levels. The result is that large predator fish, such as tuna, swordfish, and sharks, often have extraordinarily high mercury concentrations in their bodies. People who eat the fish absorb the mercury, and it builds up in their body tissue. Because the greatest risk is to developing babies in the womb, the FDA warns pregnant or nursing women not to consume any shark or swordfish and to limit their diets to no more than two servings of other types of fish per week.

> " Researchers learned that over time, the children lost their ability to excrete the mercury in their urine, which caused it to build up in their body tissues. "

Some scientists are convinced that mercury in children's body tissues can lead to autism. This is the perspective of Boyd Haley, who heads the chemistry department at the University of Kentucky and is an expert on mercury toxicity. Haley says that the connection between mercury and autism is one that needs to be aggressively pursued and that government research has not adequately determined the many different sources of mercury, or the amount of damage it can cause. He cites a study that was done in an orphanage in Portugal that examined the neurological effects of placing dental amalgams, or silver fillings that contain mercury, in children. Researchers learned that over time, the children lost their ability to excrete the mercury in their urine, which caused it to build up in their body tissues. Haley notes that this was even more signifi cant in boys, who were much less able to excrete the mercury than girls. "It is well known that many more boys

> **Contrary to what is often believed, many scientists, physicians, parents, and others who urge caution in the use of childhood vaccinations are not against vaccines.**

in the USA have autism and other neurological illnesses than do girls," he says. "It seems reasonable that the ability of girls to excrete mercury better plays a major role in the higher ratio of boys with neurological problems. It also fits into our observations that testosterone (male hormone) enhances the toxicity of [mercury] to neurons in culture whereas estrogen (female hormone) offers significant protection."[31]

Mercury Use in Vaccines

A particularly contentious debate relates to the use of mercury-based thimerosal as a preservative in childhood vaccines. In 1999 the FDA stated that "depending on the vaccine formulations used and the weight of the infant, some infants could have been exposed to cumulative levels of mercury during the first six months of life that exceeded EPA [Environmental Protection Agency] recommended guidelines for safe intake." In October 2001 the Immunization Safety Review Committee concluded that the evidence was inadequate to either accept or reject a causal relationship between thimerosal exposure from childhood vaccines and autism. The committee acknowledged, however, that the possibility of thimerosal-containing vaccines being associated with neuro-developmental disorders was "biologically plausible" and concluded that the removal of thimerosal from vaccines was "a prudent measure in support of the public health goal to reduce mercury exposure of infants and children as much as possible."[32] Today most routinely recommended vaccines contain no thimerosal or only trace amounts.

Despite the government's assurance that thimerosal is safe for children, many people remain unconvinced. Haley says there is no doubt that the preservative is dangerous, as he explains:

> You couldn't even construct a study that shows thimerosal is safe. It's just too darn toxic. If you inject thimerosal into an animal it will become neurologically and systemically ill or die. If you apply it to living tissue, the cells die. If you put it in a petri dish, the culture dies. Knowing these things, it would be shocking if one could inject it into an infant without causing some damage. . . . The bottom line is that infants are much more susceptible to the toxic effects of thimerosal than are older children, and the placement of thimerosal into pediatric vaccines and the injection of this compound into day old infants, or even infants several months old, should have been recognized by the CDC as a dangerous, toxic practice.[33]

Haley cites a tragic, and inadvertent, incident that occurred during the 1970s at a Canadian hospital. Thimerosal, in the form of a reddish-colored antiseptic solution known as Merthiolate, was applied to 13 newborns who had infected umbilical cords. Merthiolate had been used for many years as a treatment for cuts and abrasions and had reportedly not caused toxic effects. But when used on the infants, 10 out of 13 died.

The Vaccine Controversy

The debate over whether childhood vaccines are linked to autism seems to grow more heated every day. A direct relationship between childhood vaccines and autism has never been proved. Marc Siegel, an internist and associate professor at New York University School of Medicine, explains: "To be sure, there is a significant increase in autism and environmental factors appear to play a role as does improved diagnostic sensitivity to autism. But in several epidemiological studies, no association between autism and thimerosal has been proven. Does this mean that no such association exists? No, it does not."[34] Most scientists, no matter which side they are on, agree that further research is necessary before accurate conclusions can be drawn. Still, between 1983 and 2007 autism rates rose from an estimated 4 or 5 out of 10,000 children to one in 150 children, and over that same period the CDC's recommended vaccine schedule rose from 10 to 36 vaccinations. Whether this is merely a coincidence or a warning sign that vaccines can lead to autism is a definite point of contention.

Contrary to what is often believed, many scientists, physicians, parents, and others who urge caution in the use of childhood vaccinations are not against vaccines. Rather, their concern is that the current schedule for inoculations is potentially harmful. That is the perspective of Hannah Poling's father, Jon Poling, who is a neurologist in Athens, Georgia. As a physician, Poling is well aware of the importance of vaccines, but he is adamant that the inoculation schedule needs to be changed. He writes:

> The current vaccine schedule, co-sponsored by the CDC and the American Academy of Pediatrics, injures a small but significant minority of children, my daughter unfortunately being one of those victims. Every day, more parents and some pediatricians reject the current vaccine schedule. In an abundance of caution, meaningful reform must be performed urgently to prevent the re-emergence of serious diseases like polio or measles. . . . Reform of the vaccine schedule will be an important part of the solution, whether vaccines play a major or minor role in autism.[35]

A 2007 study commissioned by the autism group Generation Rescue showed that vaccinated children were 2.5 times more likely to have autism or other neurological disorders than nonvaccinated children were. The survey, which was the first of its kind, compared 9,000 boys aged 4 to 17 in certain counties of California and Oregon and found that those who were vaccinated were 224 percent more likely to have attention deficit hyperactivity disorder (ADHD) and 61 percent more likely to have autism. This was even more pronounced among the boys in the 11 to 17 age bracket: Vaccinated boys were 317 percent more likely to have ADHD and 112 percent more likely to have autism.

Will Autism's Cause Remain Elusive?

Is autism the result of environmental pollution? Is it caused by mercury poisoning, or by too many vaccinations in too short of a time? Although there are many theories, these questions remain unanswered. The only certainty is that autism remains a mysterious disorder that is not fully understood—and as the number of autism cases continues to climb, scientists grow even more determined to find the cause.

What Causes Autism?

66 I think there's a real concern that there's been a change in our environment. An exposure to some toxins, chemicals, environmental factors—either when a mother is pregnant or after the delivery of the child—that has led to autism.99

—Carol Berkowitz, "Is Autism in the Genes? Or the Environment?" *Today*, MSNBC, February 23, 2005. www.msnbc.msn.com.

Berkowitz is president of the American Academy of Pediatrics.

66 Autism is one of the most heritable complex disorders, with compelling evidence for genetic factors and little or no support for environmental influence.99

—Jeremy Veenstra-VanderWeele, Susan L. Christian, and Edwin H. Cook Jr., "Autism as a Paradigmatic Complex Genetic Disorder," *Annual Review of Genomics and Human Genetics*, September 2004. http://arjournals.annualreviews.org.

Veenstra-VanderWeele, Christian, and Cook are with the University of Chicago Department of Psychiatry.

Bracketed quotes indicate conflicting positions.

* Editor's Note: While the definition of a primary source can be narrowly or broadly defined, for the purposes of Compact Research, a primary source consists of: 1) results of original research presented by an organization or researcher; 2) eyewitness accounts of events, personal experience, or work experience; 3) first-person editorials offering pundits' opinions; 4) government officials presenting political plans and/or policies; 5) representatives of organizations presenting testimony or policy.

Primary Source Quotes

> ❝The CDC paid the Institute of Medicine to conduct a new study to whitewash the risks of thimerosal, ordering researchers to 'rule out' the chemical's link to autism.❞

—Robert F. Kennedy Jr., "Deadly Immunity," *Rolling Stone*, June 20, 2005. www.rollingstone.com.

Kennedy is an environmental attorney and writer from New York City.

> ❝I am concerned that all the attention paid to thimerosal takes the focus away from a much larger issue: *We Don't Know* why autism is on the rise. Too much thimerosal-mongering distracts us from a true scientific investigation of what is really causing all the autism.❞

—Marc Siegel, "Debating the Causes of Autism," *Nation*, August 15, 2005. www.thenation.com.

Siegel is an internist and associate professor at New York University School of Medicine.

> ❝I am very much opposed to the routine vaccination schedule in the U.S. There are too many vaccines given too early in a child's life and not enough information given to parents.❞

—Jay Gordon, "Dr. Jay's Frequently Asked Questions." www.drjaygordon.com.

Gordon is a well-known pediatrician from Los Angeles.

> ❝Even though there is ABSOLUTELY NO EVIDENCE that thimerosal or the [measles, mumps, and rubella vaccine] causes autism, there are thousands of Internet sites that dispute it.❞

—Rod Moser, "AAARGH! Childhood Vaccines Do NOT Cause Autism!" WebMD, September 18, 2007. http://blogs.webmd.com.

Moser is a primary care physician assistant from Roseville, California.

❝The rise of [autism], which shows up before age 3, happens to coincide with the increased number and type of vaccine shots in the first few years of life. So as a trigger, vaccines carry a ring of both historical and biological plausibility.❞

—Bernadine Healy, "Fighting the Autism-Vaccine War," *U.S. News & World Report*, April 21, 2008.

Healy, the former director of the National Institutes of Health, is health editor for *U.S. News & World Report* and a member of the President's Council of Advisors on Science and Technology.

❝Most research suggests that parents are confusing correlation with causation—the symptoms of autism just happen to emerge at the about the same time as recommended vaccinations are given. It's a coincidence, not a cause.❞

—Ronald Bailey, "Polio, Autism, or Neither?" *Reason*, July 24, 2006. www.reason.com.

Bailey is a science correspondent for *Reason* magazine and Reason.com.

❝The most contentious issue of the autism debate is the link to routine childhood vaccines. My daughter's case, *Hanna Poling v. U.S. Department of Health and Human Services*, has changed this debate forever.❞

—Jon S. Poling, "Father: Child's Case Shifts Autism Debate, *Atlanta Journal-Constitution*, April 11, 2008. www.ajc.com.

Poling's daughter Hannah developed autism soon after getting vaccinations and received a financial settlement from the U.S. government.

❝We can now say, from multiple independent lines of evidence, that vaccines do not cause autism.❞

—Steven Novella, "Vaccines and Autism: Myths and Misconceptions," *Skeptical Inquirer*, November/December 2007. www.csicop.org.

Novella is an assistant professor of neurology at Yale University School of Medicine.

66 There are perhaps hundreds of different causes, and I think the field is finally coming to grips with that.99

—Dan Geschwind, quoted in Mary Carmichael, "A Terrible Mystery: New Clues and New Questions in the Hunt for a Cause," *Newsweek*, November 27, 2006.

Geschwind is a neurogeneticist at the University of California, Los Angeles.

66 There's a lot of disagreement among autism practitioners and researchers about just what it is. The consensus would be that it's at least in part genetically determined. I think there's consensus on that. But beyond that—no.99

—David Wilder, quoted in Tom Spears, "What Causes Autism?" *Ottawa Citizen*, September 30, 2007. www.canada.com.

Wilder is a psychologist at Florida Institute of Technology.

Facts and Illustrations

What Causes Autism?

- Research has shown that if one identical twin is autistic, the other has a **60 to 91 percent** chance of also having autism.

- Researchers believe that between **5 and 15 genes** may be related to autism.

- **Thimerosal** was first used as a preservative in vaccines in the 1930s, before the FDA existed.

- In 2005 the Immunization Safety Review Committee concluded that there was insufficient evidence to either accept or reject a causal relationship between **thimerosal in vaccines and autism in children**.

- Thimerosal is no longer used as a preservative in most childhood vaccines.

- A 2007 study conducted by Generation Rescue showed that vaccinated boys were as much as **112 percent** more likely to develop autism than nonvaccinated boys.

- A study performed in California and Pennsylvania showed that autism in certain counties correlated with the **expansion of cable television**.

- A study conducted in Israel during 2006 showed that children who were fathered by men aged 40 or older were **6 times more likely to be autistic** as those with fathers under 30.

A Mysterious Disorder

Scientists have many theories about what causes autism, but at this point, they are only theories. In general, it is believed that autism is a genetic condition that can be triggered by numerous factors such as immune system deficiencies, exposure to environmental toxins, hormonal dysfunction, and brain inflammation. This illustration shows how these various factors come together and might interrelate to cause autism.

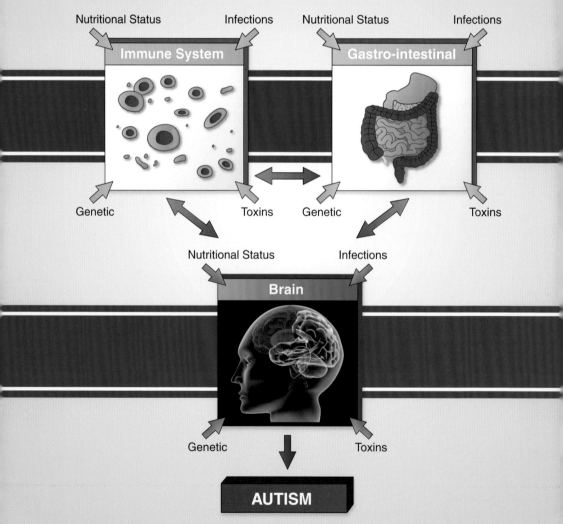

Source: "Overview of Biomedical Intervention Treatments and Services," Autism Treatment Trust. www.autismtrust.org.uk.

Autism Risk Rises with Age of Parents

Although it is an issue of controversy, several studies have shown that the older parents are, the greater their risk for having an autistic child. This graph shows the results of a study published April 2007, which was performed by Kaiser Permanente and involved more than 132,000 children, 593 of whom were diagnosed with an autism spectrum disorder.

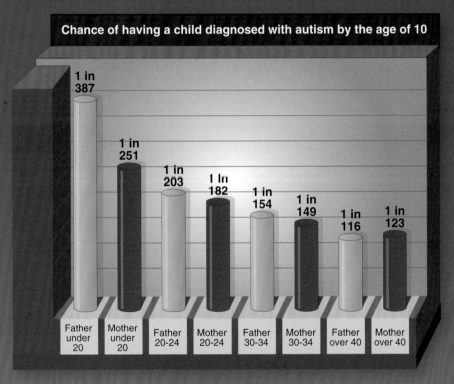

Chance of having a child diagnosed with autism by the age of 10

1 in 387	1 in 251	1 in 203	1 in 182	1 in 154	1 in 149	1 in 116	1 in 123
Father under 20	Mother under 20	Father 20-24	Mother 20-24	Father 30-34	Mother 30-34	Father over 40	Mother over 40

Source: Lisa A. Croen, "Maternal and Paternal Age and Risk of Autism Spectrum Disorders," *Archives of Pediatrics and Adolescent Medicine*, April 2007, pp. 334–40.

- In 1983 the CDC recommended **10 vaccines** for children under the age of 5; by 2007 the number had grown to **36**.

- Public studies in Texas showed that the largest increase in autism rates occurred in counties that had the most **discharge of industrial waste**.

Vaccines and Autism

In terms of autism and its causes, there is no more contentious debate than whether childhood vaccines either trigger autism or exacerbate its severity. One fact cannot be argued, though: during the same period of time that autism rates in the United States have spiked, the number of recommended vaccines has increased from 10 in 1983 to 36 in 2008. Although the CDC, the American Academy of Pediatrics, the FDA, and other agencies reject the notion that there is a connection, thousands of parents, along with a number of physicians, scientists, and autism organizations such as Generation Rescue, believe that they are wrong. This illustration shows the CDC's recommended vaccine schedule from 1983 compared with today.

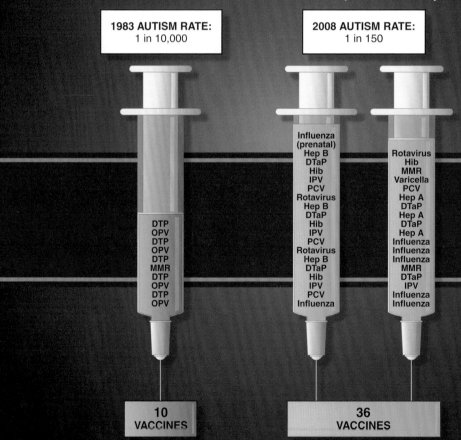

1983 AUTISM RATE:
1 in 10,000

2008 AUTISM RATE:
1 in 150

DTP
OPV
DTP
OPV
DTP
MMR
DTP
OPV
DTP
OPV

Influenza
(prenatal)
Hep B
DTaP
Hib
IPV
PCV
Rotavirus
Hep B
DTaP
Hib
IPV
PCV
Rotavirus
Hep B
DTaP
Hib
IPV
PCV
Influenza

Rotavirus
Hib
MMR
Varicella
PCV
Hep A
DTaP
Hep A
DTaP
Hep A
Influenza
Influenza
Influenza
MMR
DTaP
IPV
Influenza
Influenza

10
VACCINES

36
VACCINES

Source: "Are We Poisoning Our Kids in the Name of Protecting Their Health?" Generation Rescue, 2008. www.generationrescue.org.

Americans' Views on Mercury in Vaccines

Beginning in the 1930s, thimerosal, which is about 50 percent mercury, was used as a preservative in many childhood vaccines. Today that is not the case, as all routinely recommended vaccines contain no thimerosal or only trace amounts. It is, however, still used in the influenza vaccine, which is often given to pregnant women and young children. In a November 2006 poll conducted by Zogby International, respondents were asked questions about mercury in vaccinations.

"Mercury should not be an ingredient in flu shots or other vaccines, especially those given to pregnant women or children."

"Congress should take action to make sure that mercury and other toxins are not in flu shots and other vaccines."

"Mercury in childhood vaccines has played a role in the current autism epidemic."

Source: Zogby International, "American's Views of Mercury in Flu Shots," November 2006. www.generationrescue.org.

How Effective Are Autism Treatments?

66You'd think that a diagnosis of autism from a quali-
fied medical professional would help settle parents'
concerns—and send them in the right direction to
help their child. Most of the time, though, that just
isn't the case.99

—Lisa Jo Rudy, "The End of Autism Awareness Month—and Predictions for the Future."

66From the moment parents absorb the shock that their
child may be autistic, they enter a dizzying world of
specialists, therapists and, alas, purveyors of snake
oil.99

—Claudia Wallis, "A Tale of Two Schools."

At one time autism was thought to be a mentally crippling disorder
with only one prognosis: hopelessness. Parents were told that their
autistic children were, and would always be, severely retarded, with
no likelihood of living normal lives. Fortunately, that is no longer a wide-
spread belief. Even though it can be extremely disturbing for parents to
hear the diagnosis of autism, there are many success stories of children
who have made remarkable progress after being treated. Steve Edelson
shares his thoughts:

A few years ago, we rarely heard of a recovery or near-recovery from autism. But in the past three years, the Autism Research Institute began receiving letters, faxes, emails and phone calls from parents and from professionals reporting recovery or near-recovery. . . . These children now play with their same-aged peers and have real friends, they are doing very well in school, their behaviors are socially and emotionally appropriate, they communicate normally, and no one suspects the child once had a potentially life-long disability.[36]

Behavior Therapy

One of the most commonly used treatments for autism is applied behavior analysis, or ABA. Developed during the 1960s by UCLA psychologist Ole Ivar Lovaas, ABA revolves around the theory that when appropriate behaviors are positively reinforced, they are more likely to be repeated than when they are ignored. During therapy sessions, which take place at home, in school, or both, tasks are broken down into small, simple steps, and when one is accomplished, the child is rewarded. A study published by Lovaas in 1987 showed that nearly half of the children who received 40 hours of ABA therapy per week were able to attend regular school classes, while those who had only 10 hours of therapy made little or no progress.

Many parents say that their autistic children have blossomed after participating in ABA therapy. One of its biggest fans is Kit Weintraub, a Monroe, Wisconsin, mother of two autistic children who is active with Families for Early Autism Treatment. According to Weintraub, both of her children developed normally until they were about two years old and then began to lose their skills. She writes:

> The sheer agony of watching one's children disappear before one's very eyes is something that no one should have to experience. My daughter was seriously self-injurious. My husband and I had to take shifts with her through the night for years because she rarely slept for more than two hours at a time. Both children screamed inconsolably for most of the day for no reason that we could understand. They were unable to communicate and miserably unhappy.[37]

After putting her children in an ABA program, she noticed that they were making wonderful progress. By the time Nicholas was 7 years old, he was mainstreamed in a regular classroom at school, his IQ had risen almost 50 points, and he was reading at the fifth-grade level. Emily was more severely autistic than her brother was, so her progress was slower. But Weintraub says that at 10 years old she was happy, spoke in clear sentences, could dress herself, and spent most of her school day in a regular classroom.

> **Even though it can be extremely disturbing for parents to hear the diagnosis of autism, there are many success stories of children who have made remarkable progress after being treated.**

ABA is not without controversy, however. Opponents say that rather than teaching autistic children to think, or to develop their own unique talents and capabilities, ABA merely teaches them to act and behave as the nonautistic world *expects* them to behave. "Autism has traditionally been seen as a shell from which a normal child might one day emerge," writes *New York Times* journalist Amy Harmon. "But some advocates contend that autism is an integral part of their identities, much more like a skin than a shell, and not one they care to shed. The effort to cure autism, they say, is not like curing cancer, but like the efforts of a previous age to cure left-handedness."[38]

Some people object to ABA because of Lovaas himself. When he first began using the therapy technique with autistic children, his focus was as much on punishment as it was on reward. In an effort to stop children from behaving inappropriately, Lovaas and his therapists used what were known as aversives—they screamed at the children, hit them, withheld food and water, and even shocked them with electricity. In a 1974 interview with journalist Paul Chance, Lovaas discussed the shock technique: "We know the shocks are painful; we have tried them on ourselves and we know that they hurt. But it is stressful for the person who does the shocking too. . . . But then when you shock him and you see the self-destructive behavior stop, it is tremendously rewarding."[39] Although such cruel tactics disappeared long ago from ABA and aversives are no longer the focus, the negative perception still lingers with those who oppose this therapy method.

The DIR (Floortime Model)

Child psychiatrist Stanley Greenspan believes that it is not enough simply to teach autistic children to perform repetitive tasks. He says they need to learn how to understand emotions so they can develop emotionally, empathize with others, build relationships, and learn to think in creative and abstract ways. Greenspan developed a program called the developmental, individual-difference, relationship-based (DIR) model, which is informally known as Floortime. Parents and/or therapists get down on the floor, enter the child's world, and let him or her take the lead in play-therapy sessions. Patricia Stacey explains the Floortime approach:

> Though it emphasized relationship, fun, joy, the method drew its power from parents' ability to entice an impaired child to perform at increasingly higher levels of attention, cognition, and motor functioning—far higher than the child would normally be disposed to. It was tailored to a child's particular deficits and strengths and designed to grow in scope as the child climbed the developmental ladder.[40]

Stacey speaks from personal experience because she found that Floortime worked amazingly well for her son, Walker. He first began exhibiting signs of autism at the age of seven months. He would not cuddle, stared off into space, would not make eye contact with his parents, and sometimes swung his head from side to side and moved his arms and legs up and down rapidly and repetitively. After meeting with Greenspan, and with the aid of several therapists trained in the Floortime method, Stacey and her husband began working with Walker. They used games that held his attention, caused him to want to interact with them, and developed his imagination and thinking skills. By the time he was three and a half years old, Walker was showing amazing progress, as Greenspan told the Staceys during a follow-up evaluation: "He's intelligent, a great problem solver, creative thinker, has a can-do attitude. More important, he's got that spark in his eye. You don't see the average kid looking this wonderful."[41]

The Son-Rise Program

In the 1970s when Raun Kaufman was 18 months old, he was diagnosed as severely autistic, with an IQ of less than 30. He did not talk, withdrew from any human contact, and spent his days engaging in repetitive behaviors such as spinning plates, rocking back and forth, and flapping his hands in front of his face. "I didn't want to be touched," he writes, "I never looked at other people, and I did not give the slightest response to the calls and requests of the people around me. I was, in every way, 'in my own world.'" Kaufman's parents were told to expect no change in their son's development; that he would never speak, never have friends, never go to school, and never learn to communicate in any meaningful way. "My condition, it was said, was incurable, unchangeable, and 'hopeless,'" he says. "The professionals recommended eventual institutionalization."[42]

Instead of accepting such a bleak prognosis, Kaufman's parents designed their own child-centered treatment called the Son-Rise Program. Son-Rise focuses on accepting the child and interacting with him or her in an enthusiastic, positive way many times throughout the day. Sessions take place in a specially designed playroom in the home, where the child feels safe and secure. Instead of expecting the child to conform to the expectations of a world that he or she cannot understand, parents and therapists are encouraged to join the child's world, and even engage in playful activities such as hand flapping and repetitive play. Kaufman explains:

> **Many parents say that their autistic children have blossomed after participating in ABA therapy.**

> We never label our children's repetitive and ritualistic behaviors as inappropriate, wrong, or bad. In fact, we do not judge any of our children's challenges—even if they don't change. At the same time, we look for the possibilities, not the deficiencies, in the children we work with. We do not put limits on the future of any child. Thus, we open the door for limitless growth and progress.[43]

Kaufman says that after his parents worked with him for about three years, he completely recovered and had no autistic traits. He graduated from high school with honors, went on to earn a degree in Biomedical Ethics from Brown University, and directed an educational center for children. Today he lectures internationally at conferences, symposia, and universities and is an author, a teacher, and the director of global outreach for the Son-Rise Program at the Autism Treatment Center of America.

> **Kaufman says that after his parents worked with him for about three years, he completely recovered and had no autistic traits.**

Treating Autism Nutritionally

Many parents of autistic children have turned to alternative treatment methods, such as feeding the children diets that are free from gluten (found in grains such as wheat and oats) and casein (found in dairy products). Scott Faber, a pediatrician at the Children's Institute in Pittsburgh, is one of many physicians who recommend a gluten- and casein-free diet for autistic patients. Faber says that although it is not a cure, the diet has led to marked improvements in behavior, attention, and communication skills in children with autism. Marla Green found this to be true with her six-year-old son, John, after she put him on the special diet. Within 24 hours she noticed improvements in his eye contact and attention span, and he began babbling. "It wasn't silent in the house anymore," she says. "It kind of woke him up."[44] Jenny McCarthy also noticed remarkable progress in her son after she switched him to a gluten- and casein-free diet.

Pets That Help Heal

Because autistic children often relate better to animals than to humans, many people use pets as part of their therapy. Jennifer Baról, a social work graduate student from New Mexico, saw the positive result of this during 2006, when she was working with a five-year-old autistic boy named Zachary. He had never spoken a complete sentence, often covered his eyes and cowered in corners, and threw tantrums when he could not make people understand him. He easily became stressed and did not know how to play.

After she started to work with Zachary, Baról embarked on a study titled "The Effects of Animal-Assisted Therapy on a Child with Autism." Her goal was to determine whether animal-assisted therapy could help increase social skills in children with autism. She introduced Zachary to Henry, an 8-year-old Australian cattle dog. The boy and dog formed a bond, and half-way through the 15-week study, Zachary spoke his first sentence and began to make amazing progress. According to Baról, the boy has been transformed into a different child. He is more aware of his surroundings and the needs of other people, is more self-assured, and is curious about new activities. She believes that bonding with Henry has opened up a new world for Zachary.

> "Unfortunately, even with the best therapy possible, some autistic children make little or no progress."

Treatments Not Always Successful

Unfortunately, even with the best therapy possible, some autistic children make little or no progress. When David Slatkin was diagnosed with severe autism at the age of 17 months, his parents started him on an ABA program for 50 hours per week, as well as trying other therapies and medications. Yet even with such intensive treatment, David did not improve. At 8 years old he still could not talk and had problems understanding language. Because he tended to wander off when he was not being watched, his parents installed locks on all the doors, high up so he could not reach them. One night they forgot to lock the kitchen door. The next morning they found it open and saw that David had smashed all the glasses on the floor. He also exhibited abusive behavior sometimes, as his mother, Laura Slatkin, explains:

> One day at the supermarket, he was in such a vile mood, lunging and scratching. When I leaned down to pick him

up, he bit my shoulder really, really hard. I couldn't disengage him except by doing the most effective thing—which was to grab his hair at the back of his head and pull hard. People saw that, and you can imagine the looks they gave me! We had to give up and leave.[45]

Slatkin and her husband have been deeply saddened over David's lack of progress, and acknowledge that their son will never be normal. "It would mean the world to . . . have David turn and say, 'I love you, Mom,' or 'I want chicken for dinner,'" she says. "It's crushing; it just takes a huge chunk out of you not to be able to communicate with your son."[46] The Slatkins fear that as David grows older and stronger, they will no longer be able to care for him and will have to send him to a special facility near Boston that specializes in children with autism.

Hope for the Future

Although autism has no one-size-fits-all treatment, many autistic children have shown excellent progress through ABA, Floortime, the Son-Rise Program, and pet therapy, while others have improved because of restrictive diets. Sadly enough, there are children who do not make progress no matter what treatment is used or how intensive it is. Scientists hope that in the future, that will no longer be the case—that someday, all autistic children will benefit from treatment and live happy, healthy lives.

How Effective Are Autism Treatments?

Primary Source Quotes

> **❝For me, the most heartbreaking part of working with families with autistic children is that modern science and modern medicine do not acknowledge the need for nutritional intervention.❞**

—Carolyn Dean and Elissa Meininger, "Autism Can Be Treated," News with Views, November 13, 2007. www.newswithviews.com.

Dean is a medical doctor and nutritionist, and Meininger is a political analyst and cofounder of Health Freedom Action Network.

> **❝It must be stressed again that the cause of autism is unknown and that dietary interventions have not been shown to improve the symptoms of children with autism.❞**

—Campion Quinn, *100 Questions & Answers About Autism: Expert Advice from a Physician/Parent Caregiver*. Sudbury, MA: Jones and Bartlett, 2006.

Quinn is a physician from Long Island, New York, whose only son was diagnosed with autism at the age of three.

Bracketed quotes indicate conflicting positions.

* Editor's Note: While the definition of a primary source can be narrowly or broadly defined, for the purposes of Compact Research, a primary source consists of: 1) results of original research presented by an organization or researcher; 2) eyewitness accounts of events, personal experience, or work experience; 3) first-person editorials offering pundits' opinions; 4) government officials presenting political plans and/or policies; 5) representatives of organizations presenting testimony or policy.

66 Doctors will tell you not to say it, but for me, he's cured. There's not a problem and he won't have a problem the rest of his life. 99

—Dan Marino, "The Marino Family's Fight Against Autism," *Today*, MSNBC, February 22, 2005. www.msnbc.msn.com.

Marino is a former quarterback with the Miami Dolphins whose autistic son made remarkable progress through early intervention and therapy.

66 We don't have a disease. So we can't be 'cured.' This is just the way we are. 99

—Jack Thomas, quoted in Amy Harmon, "How About Not 'Curing' Us, Some Autistics Are Pleading," *New York Times*, December 20, 2004. www.nytimes.com.

Thomas is a young autistic man who is an activist on behalf of others with autism.

66 Autism was once thought an 'incurable' disorder, but that notion is crumbling in the face of knowledge and understanding that is increasing even as you read this. 99

—Ellen Notbohm, *Ten Things Every Child with Autism Wishes You Knew*. Arlington, TX: Future Horizons, 2005.

Notbohm, the mother of an autistic child, is the author of numerous books on autism and a columnist for *Autism-Asperger's Digest* and *Children's Voice*.

66 Currently, there are no effective means to prevent autism, no fully effective treatments, and no cure. 99

—Autism Speaks, "What Is Autism? An Overview." www.autismspeaks.org.

Autism Speaks seeks to raise awareness of autism and to raise money to fund scientific and biomedical research.

> 66 The Federal Government and several multi-million dollar autism groups hope to be 'finding effective drugs for the symptoms of autism' in 7 to 10 years. NONSENSE! We need to tell them, and the media, and the tens of thousands of families of autistic children who don't know, that many effective treatments are available NOW. 99

—Autism Research Institute, "Autism Is Treatable!" www.autism.com.

The Autism Research Institute conducts scientific research designed to improve the methods of diagnosing, treating, and preventing autism.

> 66 It's such a puzzle that, even though we know autism is a biological disorder, right now our only treatments are behavioral or educational. 99

—Sally J. Rogers, "Welcome Message," Autism Phenome Project (APP), University of California, Davis. www.ucdmc.ucdavis.edu.

Rogers is a professor in the Department of Psychiatry and Behavioral Sciences at the University of California, Davis School of Medicine.

> 66 Despite the obviously good results we are achieving, there are a great many obstacles to overcome. One major obstacle is the obstinate insistence by the Food and Drug Administration that there is no effective treatment for autism, and that it is quackery to claim otherwise. 99

—Bernard Rimland, "Autism *Is* Treatable!" November 19, 2003. www.autism.com.

Rimland, who died in 2006, was the father of an autistic son and founder of the Autism Society of America.

66 Parents . . . need to be realistic. There is no cure, but there are behavioral treatments that have been shown to be effective in improving the condition. **99**

—Laura Schreibman, quoted in Scott LaFee, "Researcher-Author Wants to Clear Up Misconceptions," *San Diego Union-Tribune*, May 24, 2006. www.signonsandiego.com.

Schreibman is a professor of psychology and director of the Autism Research Program at the University of California, San Diego.

66 Sara was diagnosed quite early and treated effectively. Today, she is nine years old and, although she still faces some challenges, she has made remarkable progress. She is one of the lucky ones. **99**

—Nancy D. Wiseman, *Could It Be Autism?* New York: Broadway, 2006.

Wiseman, the mother of an autistic girl, is founder and president of First Signs, Inc.

66 Although early intervention has a dramatic impact on reducing symptoms and increasing a child's ability to grow and learn new skills, it is estimated that *only 50% of children are diagnosed before kindergarten.* **99**

—Margaret Strock, "Autism Spectrum Disorders," National Institute of Mental Health. www.nimh.nih.gov.

Strock is with the NIMH Office of Communications.

How Effective Are Autism Treatments?

- A study published in 1987 showed that nearly **50 percent** of the children who participated in applied behavior analysis (ABA) therapy for 40 or more hours per week were later able to attend regular school classes.

- When ABA therapy was first developed, a key component was known as **aversives: yelling, hitting, and electric shocks.**

- Today **ABA** is the most common therapy used to treat autistic children.

- Research has shown that the **immune system** plays a critical role in some types of autism; therefore, if the immune system can be repaired, autistic symptoms can be minimized.

- During a study in 2007 researchers found that they could **reverse signs of autism** in mice by using drugs to activate a gene known as MECP2.

- Although research has shown autism treatments are most effective when diagnosed early, only about **50 percent** of children are diagnosed before they enter kindergarten.

- Hundreds of parents say that **chelation** has rid their children of autistic symptoms, but there is no scientific evidence to support that the treatment, which eliminates dangerous toxins from the body, works.

- In a study during 2006, chemist James Adams found that **chelation rids children of heavy metals** that had built up in their bodies; afterward, their parents saw improvements in their behavior.

- Autism treatments can cost as much as **$100,000 per year**, so many people are not able to afford them.

Most Common Treatments for Autism

There are numerous options for treating autism, and as diagnoses continue to climb, new treatments will undoubtedly become available. This table, prepared by the Interactive Autism Network (IAN), shows the top 14 treatments as reported by parents as of February 2008.

1. Prescription Medications (such as Risperdal or antidepressants)
2. Speech and Language Therapy
3. Occupational Therapy
4. Applied Behavior Analysis (ABA) and Related Therapies
5. Treatment for Sensory Integration Dysfunction (includes sensory integration therapy, use of weighted blankets or vests, deep-pressure therapy, and brushing techniques)
6. Casein/Dairy-Free and/or Gluten-Free Diet
7. Social Skills Group
8. Picture Exchange Communication Systems
9. Visual Schedules
10. Essential Fatty Acids
11. Physical Therapy
12. Social Stories
13. Developmental Individual Differences, Relationship-Based Approach (Floortime)
14. Melatonin (natural sleep aid)

Source: "Treatments Used by IAN Families (Table 2)," *IAN Research Report #5*, February 26, 2008. www.iancommunity.org.

Public Schools Pay for Most Autism Treatment

Treating autism can be extremely expensive, costing from $50,000 to more than $100,000 per year, depending on the kind of treatments and how intensive they are. Data provided to the Interactive Autism Network (IAN) as of January 2008 by more than 2,000 parents of autistic children showed how the therapy was paid for.

Breakdown of Funding

2%
Other public funding

13%
Early intervention program funds or provides

66%
Public school funds and/or provides

19%
No public funding

Source: "Treatments Used by IAN Families (Table 2)," *IAN Research Report #5*, February 26, 2008. www.iancommunity.org.

- A study released in April 2008 by Temple University researchers showed that autistic children who were treated with **sensory integration therapy** exhibited **fewer autistic mannerisms** (such as hand flapping, making noises, or having highly restricted interests) than children who received standard treatments.

The Effect of Diet on Autism

Although it has never been proven in any official scientific study, thousands of parents say that when they put their children on special diets, autistic symptoms improved or even disappeared. Following are the results of a survey of more than 26,000 parents conducted by the Autism Research Institute and published on its Web site during February 2008.

Gluten-/Casein-free diet

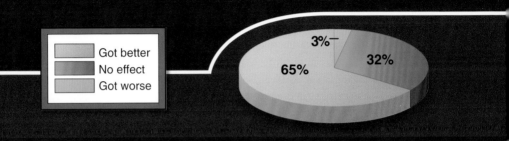

Got better
No effect
Got worse

3%
32%
65%

Candida diet
(used to eliminate yeast overgrowth in the bowels)

3%
54%
44%

Got better
No effect
Got worse

Feingold diet
(without food additives such as artificial flavoring, coloring, and sweeteners)

Got better
No effect
Got worse

2%
53%
45%

Source: "Parent Ratings of Behavioral Effects of Biomedical Interventions," Autism Research Institute, February 2008. www.autism.com.

Chelation More Effective than Ritalin

Chelation, which involves using creams, oral medications, or intravenous treatments to rid the body of metals, is only approved by the FDA for treating lead poisoning and is highly controversial as a treatment for autism. Still, numerous parents and scientists, who are convinced that autism is caused by heavy metal poisoning, swear by the treatment, saying that it has achieved remarkable results in many children and has basically cured them. In a survey by the Autism Research Institute, parents of autistic children were asked to compare results of chelation with treatment with Ritalin, an amphetamine-like drug often prescribed to treat various disorders in children. These pie charts show the answers of those parents who responded.

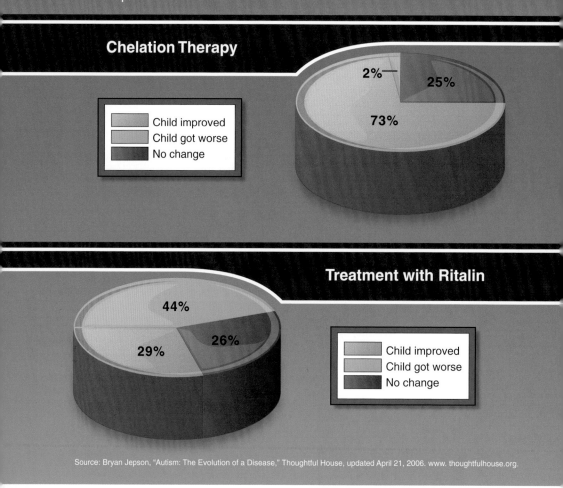

Chelation Therapy

- Child improved
- Child got worse
- No change

2% — 25%
73%

Treatment with Ritalin

44%
29% 26%

- Child improved
- Child got worse
- No change

Source: Bryan Jepson, "Autism: The Evolution of a Disease," Thoughtful House, updated April 21, 2006. www.thoughtfulhouse.org.

Will New Research Prevent or Cure Autism?

> 66 Low-functioning [autistic] people are just trying to get through the day without hurting, tapping, flailing, biting, screaming, etc. The thought of a gold pot of a potion with a cure really would be wonderful. 99

—Sue Rubin, "Acceptance versus Cure."

> 66 Although autism has traditionally been considered incurable, the 'incurability' is merely an assumption—it has never been scientifically proven. 99

—Martha R. Herbert, "Time to Get a Grip."

In October 2007 the United States Senate unanimously passed a piece of legislation that parents, scientists, and autism advocacy organizations hailed as a crucial step in the fight against autism. Known as the Combating Autism Act, the bill allocated nearly $1 billion in federal funds to be used for autism research and programs. It authorized the development of a national public awareness campaign designed to educate parents about ASDs, as well as the establishment of screening programs in all 50 states to assist with early diagnosis and intervention. "It's a huge day," says Alison Singer, who is an executive with Autism Speaks and the mother of a nine-year-old autistic girl. "I think this is the most important thing we could do short of finding a cure."[47]

Breakthrough Genetic Research

Scientists have long suspected that autism has genetic roots, but trying to determine which genes are the culprits has been a massive challenge. "It's like trying to find a few dozen innocent looking criminals in a crowd of millions,"[48] writes science journalist Bill Blakemore. In 2002 more than 120 scientists from 50 different institutions in 19 countries began working together on the largest autism genetics study that had ever been conducted: the Autism Genome Project. It involved nearly 1,200 families worldwide in which at least 2 members had an ASD, and its goal was to gain a more in-depth understanding of the relationship between autism and genetics.

DNA, which is an individual's unique genetic code, is contained in cells in the form of chromosomes that are made up of strings of genes. Using DNA samples collected from family members, the researchers analyzed the samples using highly sophisticated computer "gene chip" technology to search for genetic commonalities among autistic people. They were seeking what was known as copy number variations, or genes that did not appear in typical pairs, but rather as either a single copy or three or more copies. In February 2007, after the first phase of the project had been completed, researchers announced that they had made several important discoveries. One was that different combinations of genes may cause the various types of autism, as well as determine whether the disorder is mild or severe. Another finding was that genes associated with autism appeared to be clustered in a region on chromosome 11, a large macromolecule of DNA found among the 23 pairs of chromosomes in human cells. Project co-researcher Stephen Scherer explains the significance of these findings: "When you identify certain genes, you can then develop genetic tests—in some cases prenatal and in some cases postnatal—because early diagnosis is crucial here. When we have this type of knowledge, we can actually think about

> Scientists have long suspected that autism has genetic roots, but trying to determine which genes are the culprits has been a massive challenge.

designing better therapies based on what we know is not happening properly in the [brain] cell. We can try and design things to make it work better."[49] Scherer adds that these types of genetic discoveries can also further research toward a cure for autism.

The second phase of the Autism Genome Project was launched in April 2007 and is expected to take three years to complete. Researchers will build on their findings from the first phase and explore in even greater depth the common and rare genetic variants that are associated with autism.

Brain Studies

Many scientists have focused their research on studies of the human brain. Although the reason is unknown, research has shown that the brains of young autistic children have unusual features, such as being bigger than those of nonautistic children. In studies during 2006 using magnetic resonance imaging (MRI) technology, neuroscientist Eric Courchesne of the Children's Hospital in San Diego found that the brains of autistic children showed abnormal growth from birth to age 2, especially in the frontal lobes. Courchesne stated that by the time the children were 4 years old, their brains were the size of an average 13-year-old.

Research performed during 2007 by Marcel Just, director of Carnegie Mellon's Center for Cognitive Brain Imaging in Pittsburgh, also revealed interesting findings. Just assigned thinking tasks to a group of autistic people from 15- to 35-years-old, and they performed the tasks as he used MRI technology to scan their brains. He was able to monitor which parts of the brain were used during the tasks, and he found that their brains were not "wired" the same way as those unaffected by autism. "One thing you see," he says, "is that [activity in] different areas is not going up and down at the same time. There's a lack of synchronization, sort of like a

> " Other studies have revealed that certain parts of the brain can become chronically inflamed, which could also be a contributor to the development of autism. "

difference between a jam session and a string quartet. In autism, each area does its own thing."[50]

Other studies have revealed that certain parts of the brain can become chronically inflamed, which could also be a contributor to the development of autism. During research in 2004 Carlos Pardo-Villamizar, a Johns Hopkins neurologist, found that the immune-responsive brain cells of patients with regressive autism contained clear signs of chronic inflammation. In 2007 Pardo-Villamizar and other researchers embarked on a pilot study to test minocycline, an anti-inflammatory antibiotic drug, on ten children from 3 to 12 years old who were diagnosed with autism and had a history of developmental regression. If the antibiotic proves to be effective, it could pave the way toward a cure for regressive autism.

> Chelation treatment is most often given in the form of a sulfur-based cream that is rubbed on the skin.

Does a Cure Already Exist?

Although it is an issue of much controversy, thousands of parents, along with some scientists and physicians, are convinced that if autism is diagnosed early enough, it can be cured by chelation. Their theory is that autism is caused by mercury and/or other toxic metals and once the toxins are removed, the children lose their autistic traits. Chelation treatment is most often given in the form of a sulfur-based cream that is rubbed on the skin, but it may also be given in the form of oral or intravenous medication. Phil DeMio, a doctor and the father of an autistic child, believes in chelation therapy and explains how it works: "The sulfur grabs onto the mercury like a magnet, so our body can excrete it. Where it would never have the ability to do that on its own without something like this."[51] Scott and Angie Shoemaker are convinced that chelation cured their son, Josh, of autism. Diagnosed as autistic when he was three years old, Josh barely spoke, was not responsive, and often spent his time spinning around in circles. When they read about chelation, they decided to try it—and within five months, his mother said it was like he left his world and came into theirs. He became responsive, started to talk, and by the time he was four years old, he exhibited no signs of autism.

Jim Adams, a chemistry professor at Arizona State University, believes that heavy metals in the body may be linked to autism. After his daughter was diagnosed with autism at the age of two and a half, he began to intensively study the disorder. He learned about a mysterious condition known as acrodynia, often called pink disease, that afflicted infants and children in the United States about a century ago. Symptoms of the disease, including social withdrawal and lack of communication, were very similar to those of autism. According to Adams, acrodynia virtually disappeared once teething powders that contained mercury were removed from the market, which strengthened his belief that mercury and autism were linked. In 2006 he studied a group of autistic children with the goal of determining the effectiveness of chelation in treating them. Working with Matt Boral of the Southwest College of Naturopathic Medicine, Adams used chelation on the children and then tested their urine samples. He found that the most severe forms of autism correlated with higher excretion of lead and mercury, leading him to conclude that a definite connection exists between autism and metals. Adams presented his findings at a conference in May 2007, during which he stated: "Finding lead or mercury in an autism victim is like finding a bullet in a homicide victim—further investigation needed for 100% certainty, but in both cases it is highly likely that one caused the other."[52] Adams ended his presentation by saying more research of this kind was urgently needed.

> **Some autistic adults fear research that could lead to a cure because they do not believe they have a disease, and they do not want to be cured.**

Because no causal relationship between heavy metals and autism has been scientifically proved, the FDA, CDC, and other government agencies denounce the use of chelation for anything except lead poisoning. But on September 7, 2006, the NIMH announced that it would conduct three major clinical studies on autism, one of which would test the efficacy and safety of chelation for children with ASDs. Susan Swedo, who leads the pediatric branch of NIMH where the studies are being conducted, explains the reason for the research: "Because chelation therapy is not specific for mercury alone, it is important to conduct a systematic, controlled trial to determine whether or not chelation therapy is beneficial or potentially harmful to children with autism."[53]

Autism as Neurodiversity

As autism advocates continue to lobby for more research funding, and scientists aggressively search for a cure for autism, another movement is steadily growing in strength: autistic adults who like themselves just the way they are. Referring to their autism as neurodiversity rather than a disorder, they want people to respect that they are different and not expect them to conform to what society believes is normal or acceptable. For them, the issue is not whether a cure will be found—but rather, whether one should be found. They fear research that could lead to a cure because they do not believe they have a disease, and they do not want to be cured.

At the heart of the issue is the assumption that autistic people are mentally retarded. Although many do have some degree of mental retardation, the prevalence of this is a source of controversy. People with autism often cannot communicate so that others can understand them, and this is commonly assumed to be an indicator of mental retardation. But according to Mike Merzenich, a professor of neuroscience at the University of California, San Francisco, who has worked with numerous autistic children, the notion that mental retardation affects as many as 75 percent of autistic people is "incredibly wrong and destructive. . . . We label them as retarded because they can't express what they know."[54]

Michelle Dawson, an autistic woman from Canada, is a well-known advocate on behalf of people with autism. She works as a researcher for Laurent Mottron, a psychiatrist who specializes in autism and whose research laboratory is located at a facility known as Hôpital Rivière-des-Prairies near Montreal. Dawson spends many hours each day on the Internet writing in her blog and corresponding with scientists, parents' groups, medical institutions, journalists, and others. Her goal is to spread the message that autistic people are misunderstood and judged unfairly. "There's such a variety of human behavior," she says. "Why is my kind wrong?"[55] Dawson and other like-minded autistic individuals often speak out against ABA therapy because they believe it is dehumanizing. They also object because the practice is often used to remove odd behaviors such as rocking and flapping, which are enjoyable and even necessary for autistic people. Dawson says that when autistic children are forced through ABA therapy to pay attention, gaze appropriately, or to make eye contact with others, this can be stressful and even painful for them.

Autism Tomorrow

As perplexing as autism is, scientists are learning more about it all the time. Studies continue to show a strong link with genetic factors, although there are probably multiple causes, and as research progresses, much more will likely be discovered. Whether there will someday be a cure is not known, although with the progress that has already been made, a cure is likely in the future. In the meantime, millions of children and adults live with autism every day. Many are locked in a world that they seem unable to get out of, while others have made amazing progress and are living happy, healthy lives. Julie Kosloski is still drawn to those who have autism, and she shares her thoughts:

> Sometimes when I see autistic children I wonder, what if there is really nothing wrong with them at all? What if some part of their brain is just so hyper-developed that it inhibits their ability to communicate? Should we presume that because they act differently from us, make strange sounds and motions, and can't talk, that they're less intelligent than we are? Who knows what's going on in their minds, and what they would tell us if they could talk to us. Someday we may know how to help them break through, and I'm thankful that there are now so many people to advocate for them. But to assume there's nothing there, no hope, is just a dreadful mistake.[56]

Will New Research
Prevent or Cure Autism?

66 The brain is so mysterious, and the disease is so baffling. It will be a slow process. But will we get there?
Absolutely. 99

—Gary Goldstein, "Expert Interviews," Autism Speaks. www.autismspeaks.org.

Goldstein is a pediatric neurologist and president of Baltimore's Kennedy Krieger
Institute.

66 In most cases, there is . . . never likely to be a magic
wand, a cure that is cheap, free of risk and, most impor-
tantly, genuinely works. In the case of autism, which
is my impairment, there is not a single treatment that
has withstood the rigours of scientific scrutiny and
yet the quacks continue to peddle their wares, selling
false hopes at the expense of self-acceptance. 99

—James Medhurst, "Why I Don't Want to Be Cured," *New Statesman*, February 16, 2007. www.newstatesman.com.

Medhurst is an autistic man who lives in the United Kingdom.

Bracketed quotes indicate conflicting positions.

* Editor's Note: While the definition of a primary source can be narrowly or broadly defined, for the purposes of Compact
Research, a primary source consists of: 1) results of original research presented by an organization or researcher; 2) eyewitness
accounts of events, personal experience, or work experience; 3) first-person editorials offering pundits' opinions; 4) government
officials presenting political plans and/or policies; 5) representatives of organizations presenting testimony or policy.

66 **We are walking toward a future of hope, a future of promise, and a future when autism is not a daily struggle for millions of families but a word for the history books.** 99

—Suzanne Wright, "'New Decade' Fundraiser Brings in over $2M," Autism Speaks, May 2006. www.autismspeaks.org.

Wright, whose grandson has autism, is the cofounder of Autism Speaks.

66 **Our understanding and treatment of autism is still pretty superficial.... Yes, our understanding and treatment has vastly improved, but it's nowhere near what I hope it will become in the next decade. ... In all the self-congratulations about how far we have come in understanding autism, we need to keep in mind how very far we still have to go.** 99

—Steven Parker, "Dr. P's Top 10 Unanswered Autism Questions," *Healthy Children*, WebMD, March 24, 2008. http://blogs.webmd.com.

Parker is a pediatrician at the Boston Medical Center.

66 **We have been working almost 10 years to get to this point. If we can find and confirm that a particular gene is involved in autism the field will explode.** 99

—Gerard Schellenberg, quoted in Bio-Medicine, "New Findings on Autism Research," August 1, 2006. www.bio-medicine.org.

Schellenberg is a researcher at the Puget Sound Veterans Affairs Medical Center and a research professor of medicine at the University of Washington.

66 **Pinpointing the culprits among the tens of thousands of possible environmental factors—everything from air pollutants to ultrasound examinations during pregnancy to multiple immunizations given to kids all at once—is a monumental problem that could take decades to solve with traditional human studies.** 99

—David Stipp, "Tracing Autism's Roots," *Fortune*, April 1, 2008. http://money.cnn.com.

Stipp is a science journalist from Boston.

66 We're hoping to really fast-track some findings and the understanding of the causes and environmental factors that could possibly be implicated in autism. 99

—Clara Lajonchere, quoted in Carl Marziali, "USC Autism Research Receives $8.4 Million Grant," Medical News Today, October 4, 2007. www.medicalnewstoday.com.

Lajonchere is a research assistant professor at the University of Southern California's Viterbi School of Engineering.

66 If a disease suddenly spikes, it seems more plausible that the increase could be reversed—if only we could find the mysterious environmental trigger. With autism, though, that hopeful scenario seems just too simple. 99

—Claudia Wallis, "Is the Autism Epidemic a Myth?" *Time*, January 12, 2007. www.time.com.

Wallis is an editor at large for *Time* magazine who often writes about health- and science-related issues.

66 Autism once meant hopelessness, but that's certainly not the story line today. It's loaded with hope. 99

—Jeffie Muntifering, quoted in Fran Smith, "Rewriting a Life Story: Treating Autism Early Can Help Save Later," *Edutopia*, March 19, 2008.

Muntifering's son, who was diagnosed with autism at the age of 3, is now 18 and an honor student and athlete in high school.

66 Autism is a 24/7 problem. The children have to be looked after all the time, and the parents tend to be exhausted and broke. 99

—Bob Wright, quoted in Diane Guernsey, "Autism's Angels," *Town & Country*, August 2006.

After Wright's grandson was diagnosed with autism, he and his wife founded the Autism Speaks organization.

66 **The biggest mistake made in the autism world is deciding ahead of time all of the things that a child will never do or accomplish. We refuse to do this. Since there is no way to see the future, the only ethical choice we have is to treat every child as if he or she can be cured and give all children a chance.** 99

—Raun K. Kaufman, quoted in Brenda Nashawaty, "International Autism Expert Raun K. Kaufman Supports American Academy of Pediatrics Recommendation for Early Testing, but Rejects Position That Autism Is Incurable," Marketwire, November 19, 2007. www.marketwire.com.

Kaufman, who was diagnosed as severely autistic when he was 18 months old, is now an international speaker, writer, and CEO of the Autism Treatment Center of America.

66 **Some children just do not get better, no matter what the intervention.** 99

—Jill Neimark, "Autism: It's Not Just in the Head," *Discover*, April 2007. http://discovermagazine.com.

Neimark is a science journalist and author who lives in New York City.

Facts and Illustrations

Will New Research Prevent or Cure Autism?

- In 2007 the Combating Autism Act was approved by the United States Senate, which allocated nearly **$1 billion** for autism research and programs.

- In the first phase of the Autism Genome Project, researchers announced that they had found links between various **chromosomes and autism**.

- A study published in January 2008 showed that autism and **schizophrenia** could be linked because the two disorders have similar gene mutations.

- Research has shown that autism is a disorder that affects primarily the white matter of the brain, the area where **nerve fibers** link diverse parts of the brain.

- Researchers have found **suspicious spots on various chromosomes of the brains** of autistic people; further studies could lead to treatments and cures.

- Scientists now know that the **brains of autistic children appear to be larger** than those of nonautistic children.

- Studies have shown that the **brains of some autistic children show in-flammation**, which could mean that they could be treated and possibly cured with antibiotics.

Autism's Economic Costs

The costs of autism to society are staggering. A study released by the Harvard School of Public Health on April 25, 2006, showed that it can cost more than $3 million to take care of one autistic person over his or her lifetime, and an estimated $35 billion annually to care for all people with autism. Yet when factoring in other services that are needed to care for the autistic, such as alternative therapies and other family out-of-pocket expenses, the true cost is likely much higher. This chart shows how autism's economic costs compare with some other conditions.

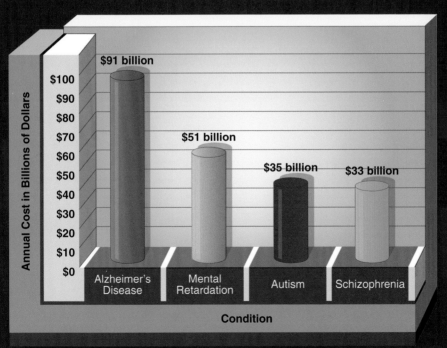

Source: "Autism Has High Costs to U.S. Society," Harvard School of Public Health, April 25, 2006. www.hsph.harvard.edu.

Brain Structures Affected by Autism

As technology becomes more advanced, researchers are learning more about the potential causes of autism, which will hopefully lead to more effective treatments and an eventual cure. Sophisticated brain imaging tools such as computerized tomography (CT), positron emission tomography (PET), single photon emission computed tomography (SPECT), and magnetic resonance imaging (MRI), have shown that many major brain structures are affected by autism.

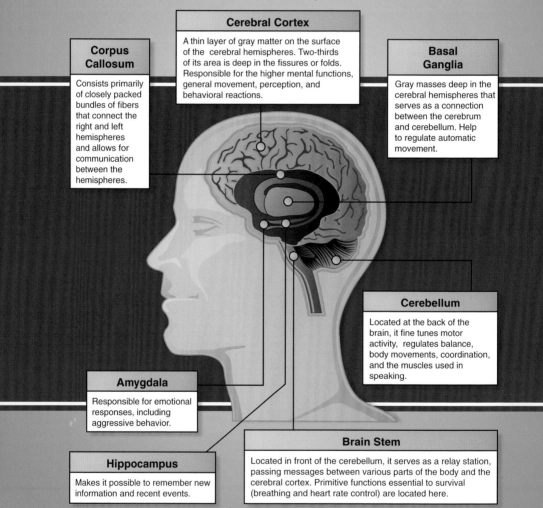

Cerebral Cortex

A thin layer of gray matter on the surface of the cerebral hemispheres. Two-thirds of its area is deep in the fissures or folds. Responsible for the higher mental functions, general movement, perception, and behavioral reactions.

Corpus Callosum

Consists primarily of closely packed bundles of fibers that connect the right and left hemispheres and allows for communication between the hemispheres.

Basal Ganglia

Gray masses deep in the cerebral hemispheres that serves as a connection between the cerebrum and cerebellum. Help to regulate automatic movement.

Cerebellum

Located at the back of the brain, it fine tunes motor activity, regulates balance, body movements, coordination, and the muscles used in speaking.

Amygdala

Responsible for emotional responses, including aggressive behavior.

Hippocampus

Makes it possible to remember new information and recent events.

Brain Stem

Located in front of the cerebellum, it serves as a relay station, passing messages between various parts of the body and the cerebral cortex. Primitive functions essential to survival (breathing and heart rate control) are located here.

Source: Margaret Strock, "Autism Spectrum Disorders," National Institute of Mental Health, updated January 2007. www.nimh.nih.gov.

Private Funding for Autism Lags Behind Other Diseases

Autism cases are spiking at an alarming rate, and it is the number-one developmental disorder. As a result, the 2007 Combating Autism Act has allocated nearly $1 billion in public funding for autism research and programs. However, private funding for autism sorely lags behind funding for other diseases and disorders.

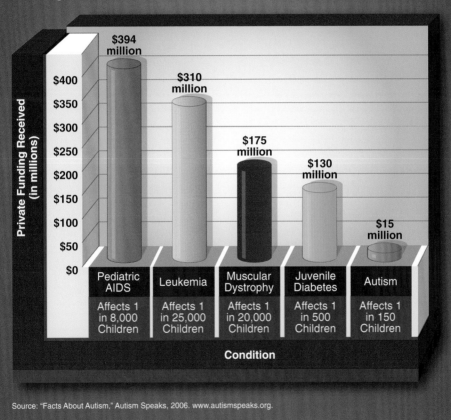

Source: "Facts About Autism," Autism Speaks, 2006. www.autismspeaks.org.

- In a 2006 study, chemist James Adams found that toxic metals such as **lead and mercury** were related to autism in children.

- In 2007 the NIMH announced that it would embark on a study to determine whether **chelation was a safe, effective treatment** for autism.

Key People and Advocacy Groups

Hans Asperger: Asperger was an Austrian pediatrician for whom the autistic disorder Asperger's syndrome is named.

Autism Research Institute: The institute conducts scientific research designed to improve the methods of diagnosing, treating, and preventing autism.

Autism Speaks: Autism Speaks seeks to increase awareness of autism spectrum disorders, fund research, and advocate for the needs of affected families.

Bruno Bettelheim: An Austrian psychotherapist, Bettelheim was influential in perpetuating the erroneous belief that autism was caused by cold, unloving mothers.

Eugen Bleuler: In 1911 Bleuler, a Swiss psychiatrist, used the word *autism* to describe adult schizophrenic patients who were socially withdrawn.

Michelle Dawson: Dawson is an autistic woman from Montreal, Canada, who advocates for the rights of autistic people.

Temple Grandin: Diagnosed as severely autistic as a child, Grandin went on to earn a PhD and became one of the most respected livestock equipment designers in the world.

Boyd Haley: Haley heads the chemistry department at the University of Kentucky and is an expert on mercury toxicity.

Leo Kanner: A psychiatrist at Johns Hopkins Hospital, Kanner introduced the term *early infantile autism* in 1943.

Ole Ivar Lovaas: During the 1960s Lovaas, a psychologist from UCLA, developed the applied behavior analysis (ABA) treatment for autism.

Jenny McCarthy: An actress and author, McCarthy says her son recovered from autism after he was detoxified and switched to a gluten- and casein-free diet.

Jon and Terry Poling: In a high-profile case about vaccines and autism, the Polings were the first to receive government compensation for their daughter's treatment.

Bernard Rimland: Rimland was the founder of the Autism Research Institute and an outspoken believer in the connection between vaccines and autism.

Sue Rubin: Diagnosed with severe autism as a child, Rubin went on to attend college and write the narration for an Oscar-nominated documentary called *Autism Is a World*.

Chronology

1911
Swiss psychiatrist Eugen Bleuler uses the word *autism* to describe adult schizophrenic patients who are socially withdrawn.

1944
Hans Asperger publishes a paper about an autism-like disorder whose symptoms are not as severe as those of autism. It is later named Asperger's syndrome.

1964
Bernard Rimland, the father of an autistic son, releases the book *Infantile Autism*, which denounces the theory that autism is caused by bad mothering.

1980
Infantile autism is included in the third release of the *Diagnostic and Statistical Manual of Mental Disorders* (DSM). The name is later changed to "autistic disorder."

1900   **1940**   **1960**   **1980**

1943
Child psychiatrist Leo Kanner publishes a paper in which he uses the term *early infantile autism* to describe a group of developmentally impaired children. He later opines that their problems are caused by cold, distant mothers.

1967
Rimland founds the Autism Research Institute. Austrian psychotherapist Bruno Bettelheim publishes *The Empty Fortress: Infantile Autism and the Birth of the Self*, in which he blames "refrigerator mothers" for childhood autism.

1970
British psychiatrist Lorna Wing develops the concept of autism spectrum disorders.

1975
The Education for All Handicapped Children Act is passed in the United States and promotes greater educational opportunities for disabled children.

1990

The Education for All Handicapped Children Act is renamed the Individuals with Disabilities Education Act, mandating a free, appropriate, publicly supported education for all children with special needs.

2002

More than 120 scientists from 50 different institutions in 19 countries begin working together on the Autism Genome Project, which is the largest autism genetics study ever conducted.

Proceedings to examine a possible link between thimerosal and autism begin in the federal vaccine court, making the first step in the legal process for parents seeking compensation for alleged adverse effects for vaccines on their children.

2008

The CDC announces that it is conducting an ongoing study in three health-care facilities in the United States to determine if exposure to thimerosal in infancy is related to autism.

2003

A CDC study finds a 10-fold increase in autism rates in Atlanta between the 1980s and 1996.

1990   2000

2008

2001

Thimerosal is removed from most regular childhood vaccines.

2005

A study done in Japan with 30,000 children shows that autism cases have continued to increase after the measles, mumps, and rubella (MMR) vaccine was replaced with single vaccines.

The first Autistic Pride Day, designed to celebrate the neurodiversity of people with autism, is held in Brazil.

2004

A joint statement issued by the AAP, American Academy of Family, physicians, the CDC vaccination advisory committee, and the Public Health Service maintains that there is no convincing evidence of harm caused by low levels of thimerosal in vaccines.

2007

The CDC announces that 1 out of every 150 children has some form of autism spectrum disorder.

In the first judgement of its kind, Jon and Terry Poling are awarded financial reimbursement for their daughter's care after convincing the vaccine court that her autism was brought on by vaccines.

The U.S. Senate passes the Combating Autism Act, which allocates nearly $1 billion in federal funds to be used for autism research and programs.

Related Organizations

Autism Research Institute (ARI)

4182 Adams Ave.

San Diego, CA 92116

toll-free phone: (866) 366-3361 • fax: (619) 563-6840

Web site: www.autism.com

The ARI, which is a worldwide network of parents and professionals, conducts scientific research designed to improve the methods of diagnosing, treating, and preventing autism. Numerous articles about autism, possible causes and triggers, treatment methods, and advances in research are available through the Web site, as are a number of video clips.

Autism Society of America (ASA)

7910 Woodmont Ave., Suite 300

Bethesda, MD 20814-3067

phone: (301) 657-0881 • toll-free: (800) 328-8476

e-mail: info@autism-society.org • Web site: www.autism-society.org

The ASA is a grassroots organization that is devoted to increasing public awareness about autism and the day-to-day issues of those who have it, advocating for appropriate services for autistic people, and providing information about treatment, education, research, and advocacy. The Web site provides information about what autism is, how it is diagnosed and treated, family issues, and resource links, as well as a free online course called Autism 101.

Autism Speaks

2 Park Ave., 11th Floor

New York, NY 10016

phone: (212) 252-8584 • fax: (212) 252-8676

e-mail: contactus@autismspeaks.org • Web site: www.autismspeaks.org

Autism Speaks is dedicated to increasing awareness of autism spectrum disorders; funding research into the causes, prevention, treatments, and cure for autism; and advocating for the needs of affected families. Available on the Web site are a number of articles, news releases, research publications, and a video glossary.

Centers for Disease Control and Prevention (CDC)

1600 Clifton Rd.

Atlanta, GA 30333

phone: (404) 498-1515 • toll-free: (800) 311-3435

fax: (800) 553-6323

e-mail: inquiry@cdc.gov • Web site: www.cdc.gov

The CDC, which is part of the U.S. Department of Health and Human Services, is charged with promoting health and quality of life by controlling disease, injury, and disability. Its Web site offers a number of informative autism-related publications and fact sheets.

Food and Drug Administration (FDA)

5600 Fishers Ln.

Rockville, MD 20857

toll-free phone: (888) 463-6332

Web site: www.fda.gov

The FDA is charged with promoting and protecting the public health by keeping products safe and effective, monitoring products for continued safety once they are in use, and providing the public with accurate, science-based information. Information available on the Web site relates to autism and vaccines, fraudulent autism treatments, and other pertinent issues.

Generation Rescue

San Francisco, CA

e-mail: info@generationrescue.org

Web site: www.generationrescue.org

Generation Rescue, which was founded by parents of children who were diagnosed with childhood neurological disorders, maintains that autism and other such disorders are caused by environmental factors and can be treated through biomedical intervention. The Web site offers numerous testimonials, studies, research papers, and surveys.

National Autism Association (NAA)

330 W. Schatz Ln.

Nixa, MO 65714

toll-free phone: (877) 622-2884

e-mail: naa@nationalautism.org

Web site: www.nationalautismassociation.org

The NAA seeks to educate and empower families who are affected by autism and other neurological disorders, as well as advocate on behalf of those who cannot fight for their own rights. Numerous materials can be found on the Web site, including an autism overview; a gallery of poetry, photos, and articles; autism myths; and a "symptoms video."

National Institute of Mental Health (NIMH)

Science Writing, Press, and Dissemination Branch

6001 Executive Blvd., Room 8184

MSC 9663

Bethesda, Maryland 20892-9663

toll-free phone: (866) 615-6464 • fax: (301) 443-4279

e-mail: nimhinfo@nih.gov • Web site: www.nimh.nih.gov

The NIMH seeks to reduce mental illness and behavioral disorders through research and supports science that will profoundly affect the diagnosis, treatment, and prevention of mental disorders. The Web site provides a wide variety of publications about autism spectrum disorders.

National Institute of Neurological Disorders and Stroke (NINDS)

PO Box 5801

Bethesda, MD 20824

phone: (301) 496-5751 • toll-free: (800) 352-9424

Web site: www.ninds.nih.gov

The NINDS is part of the National Institutes of Health, and its mission is to reduce the burden of neurological disease throughout the world through research and education. Its Web site offers many research papers and fact sheets related to autism.

Talk About Curing Autism (TACA)

PO Box 12409

Newport Beach, CA 92658-2409

phone: (949) 640-4401 • fax: (949) 640-4424

Web site: www.talkaboutcuringautism.org

The TACA provides information, resources, and support to families who are affected by autism. Its Web site offers general information about autism, statistics, an e-newsletter, a wide variety of support materials for parents of autistic children, and a "Hope After Diagnosis" video.

For Further Research

Books

Robert Evert Cimera, *Making Autism a Gift*. Lanham, MD: Rowman & Littlefield, 2007.

Barbara Firestone, *Autism Heroes*. London and Philadelphia: Jessica Kingsley, 2008.

Carol Fredericks, ed., *Perspectives on Diseases and Disorders: Autism*. Detroit: Greenhaven, 2008.

Bryan Jepson, Katie Wright, and Jane Johnson, *Changing the Course of Autism: A Scientific Approach for Parents and Physicians*. Boulder, CO: Sentient, 2007.

Jenny McCarthy, *Louder than Words: A Mother's Journey in Healing Autism*. New York: Dutton, 2007.

John T. Neisworth and Pamela S. Wolfe, *The Autism Encyclopedia*. Baltimore: Paul H. Brookes, 2005.

Ellen Notbohm, *Ten Things Every Child with Autism Wishes You Knew*. Arlington, TX: Future Horizons, 2005.

Campion Quinn, *100 Questions and Answers About Autism*. Sudbury, MA: Jones and Bartlett, 2006.

William Stillman, *The Soul of Autism: Looking Beyond Labels to Unveil Spiritual Secrets of the Heart Savants*. Franklin Lakes, NJ: New Page, 2008.

Carol Turkington and Ruth Anan, *The Encyclopedia of Autism Spectrum Disorders*. New York: Facts On File, 2007.

Nancy D. Wiseman, *Could It Be Autism?* New York: Broadway, 2006.

Periodicals

Sharon Begley, "The Puzzle of Hidden Ability," *Newsweek*, August 20, 2007.

Mary Carmichael, "A Terrible Mystery," *Newsweek*, November 27, 2006.

Sharon Cotliar, "Autism & Vaccines: One Family's Victory," *People Weekly*, March 24, 2008.

Mary Ellen Egan, "A Costly Education," *Forbes*, April 9, 2007.

Jeff Evans, "Some Do Recover from Autistic Spectrum Disorder," *Family Practice News*, May 15, 2006.

Joanne Fowler, "'Would I Trade in My Autism? No,'" *People Weekly*, May 8, 2006.

Diane Guernsey, "Autism's Angels," *Town & Country*, August 2006.

Bernadine Healy, "Fighting the Autism-Vaccine War," *U.S. News & World Report*, April 21, 2008.

Martha R. Herbert, "Time to Get a Grip," *Autism Advocate*, fifth edition, 2006.

Barbara Kantrowitz and Julie Scelfo, "What Happens When They Grow Up," *Newsweek*, November 27, 2006.

David Kirby, "Evading the Evidence," *Mothering*, March/April 2008.

Melissa Klein, "All About Autism: The Developmental Disorder Is on the Rise," *Current Health 2: A Weekly Reader Publication*, October 2007.

Melinda Marshall, "Understanding Autism," *Parenting*, April 2007.

Jill Neimark, "Autism: It's Not Just in the Head," *Discover*, April 2007.

Ronnie Polaneczky, "In His Own World," *Good Housekeeping*, May 2006.

Nancy Rones, "Losing My Little Boy," *Redbook*, February 2008.

Nathan Seppa, "Problem Paternity: Older Men Seem More Apt to Have Autistic Kids," *Science News*, September 9, 2006.

Nancy Shute, "Autism's Many Meanings," *U.S. News & World Report*, January 15, 2007.

———, "Finding Music in Autism," *U.S. News & World Report*, April 7, 2008.

Angie Smibert, "The Boy Who Spoke in Colors," *Odyssey*, December 2007.

Claudia Wallis, "Blame It on Teletubbies," *Time*, October 30, 2006.

——— "Inside the Autistic Mind," *Time*, May 7, 2006.

Internet Sources

Mark Cohen, "The Boy Who Stopped Talking," *Discover*, April 2006. http://discovermagazine.com/2006/apr/vital-signs.

Wayne Drehs, "J-Mac's Meaningful Message for Autism," ESPN, June 14, 2006. http://sports.espn.go.com/espn/news/story?id=2352763.

Amy Harmon, "How About Not 'Curing' Us, Some Autistics Are Pleading," *New York Times*, December 20, 2004. www.nytimes.com/2004/12/20/health/20autism.html?_r=1&oref=slogin.

Liz Hayes, "Autism Treatments Range from Therapy to Diets," *Pittsburgh Tribune-Review*, May 2, 2005. www.pittsburghlive.com/x/pittsburghtrib/s_330159.html.

Robert F. Kennedy Jr., "Deadly Immunity," *Rolling Stone*, June 20, 2005. www.rollingstone.com/politics/story/7395411/deadly_immunity.

Jenny McCarthy, "The Day I Heard My Son Had Autism," CNN.com, March 28, 2008. www.cnn.com/2007/US/09/24/jenny.autism/index.html?iref=newssearch.

Lisa Jo Rudy, "Symptoms, Diagnosis of Autism," About.com. http://autism.about.com/od/whatisautism/u/symptomsdiagnosis.htm.

Katherine Seligman, "Chronicles in Autism—a Boy Recovers: Can Children Be Cured?" *San Francisco Chronicle*, November 13, 2005. www.sfgate.com/cgi-bin/article.cgi?f=/c/a/2005/11/13/CMGI7F9T5N1.DTL&type=health.

Margaret Strock, "Autism Spectrum Disorders," National Institute of Mental Health. www.nimh.nih.gov/health/publications/autism/nimhautismspectrum.pdf.

Stephanie Watson, "How Autism Works," How Stuff Works. http://health.howstuffworks.com/autism.htm.

Jane Weaver, "Inside the Autism Treatment Maze," MSNBC, August 9, 2005. www.msnbc.msn.com/id/6948119.

Source Notes

Autism: An Overview

1. Robert Evert Cimera, *Making Autism a Gift*. Lanham, MD: Rowman & Littlefield, 2007, p. 5.
2. Quoted in Diane Guernsey, "Autism's Angels," *Town & Country*, August 2006, p. 95.
3. JC, "Autism Denial: Who Really Hurts from It?" Associated Content, January 6, 2007. www.associatedcontent.com.
4. Quoted in Nancy Rones, "Losing My Little Boy," *Redbook*, February 2008, p. 152.
5. Quoted in CNN.com, "Autism: What You Should Know," March 28, 2008. www.cnn.com.
6. Claudia Wallis, "Inside the Autistic Mind," *Time*, May 7, 2006. www.time.com.
7. Trisha Macnair, "Spotting Autism in a Child," BBC, October 2007. www.bbc.co.uk.
8. Jenny McCarthy, "The Day I Heard My Son Had Autism," CNN.com, September 24, 2007. www.cnn.com.
9. Margaret Strock, "Autism Spectrum Disorders," National Institute of Mental Health. www.nimh.nih.gov.
10. Quoted in Barbara Firestone, *Autism Heroes*. London and Philadelphia: Jessica Kingsley, 2008, p. 124.
11. Quoted in Jane Weaver, "Inside the Autism Treatment Maze," MSNBC, August 9, 2005. www.msnbc.msn.com.
12. Temple Grandin, PhD. www.templegrandin.com.
13. James Medhurst, "Why I Don't Want to Be Cured," *New Statesman*, February 16, 2007. www.newstatesman.com.

What Is Autism?

14. Julie Kosloski, interview with author, April 23, 2008.
15. Firestone, *Autism Heroes*, p. 3.
16. Quoted in CNN.com, "Encore Presentation: Autism Is a World," December 3, 2006. http://transcripts.cnn.com.
17. Kosloski, interview.
18. Patricia Stacey, "Floor Time," *Atlantic Monthly*, January/February 2003, p. 128.
19. Alan Hope, e-mail interview with author, April 29, 2008.
20. Hope, interview.
21. Quoted in Firestone, *Autism Heroes*, p. 10.
22. Quoted in Wallis, "Inside the Autistic Mind."
23. Quoted in Lisa Barrett Mann, "Oscar Nominee: Documentary or Fiction?" *Washington Post*, February 22, 2005. www.washingtonpost.com.
24. Kosloski, interview.

What Causes Autism?

25. Quoted in *Time*, "The Child Is Father," July 25, 1960. www.time.com.
26. National Institutes of Health, "Autism Overview: What Causes Autism?" October 8, 2007. www.nichd.nih.gov.
27. Quoted in Melissa Marino, "Gene Variant Carries Increased Risk of Autism," Kennedy Center for Research on Human Development, October 17, 2006. http://kc.vanderbilt.edu.
28. Martha R. Herbert, "Time to Get a Grip," *Autism Advocate*, fifth edition, 2006, p. 19.
29. Herbert, "Time to Get a Grip," p. 19.
30. Daniel J. DeNoon, "Mercury in Air Pollution: A Link to Autism?" Fox News, March 21, 2005. www.foxnews.com.

31. Boyd E. Haley, e-mail interview with author, April 30, 2008.

32. Food and Drug Administration, "Thimerosal in Vaccines: Frequently Asked Questions." www.fda.gov.

33. Haley, interview.

34. Marc Siegel, "Debating the Causes of Autism," *Nation*, August 15, 2005. www.thenation.com.

35. Jon S. Poling, "Father: Child's Case Shifts Autism Debate," *Atlanta Journal-Constitution*, April 11, 2008. www.ajc.com.

How Effective Are Autism Treatments?

36. Steve Edelson, "Director's Message," Autism Research Institute. www.autism.com.

37. Quoted in *Schafer Autism Report*, "Letter to the *New York Times* from Kit Weintraub." www.sarnet.org.

38. Amy Harmon, "How About Not 'Curing' Us, Some Autistics Are Pleading," *New York Times*, December 20, 2004. www.nytimes.com.

39. Quoted in Paul Chance, "After You Hit a Child, You Can't Just Get Up and Leave Him; You Are Hooked to That Kid," *Psychology Today*, January 1974, p. 80.

40. Stacey, "Floor Time," p. 130.

41. Quoted in Stacey, "Floor Time," p. 134.

42. Raun Kaufman, "The Journey Out of Autism," Autism Today. www.autism today.com.

43. Kaufman, "The Journey Out of Autism."

44. Quoted in Liz Hayes, "Autism Treatments Range from Therapy to Diets," *Pittsburgh Tribune-Review*, May 2, 2005. www.pittsburghlive.com.

45. Quoted in Guernsey, "Autism's Angels," p. 92.

46. Quoted in Guernsey, "Autism's Angels," p. 92.

Will New Research Prevent or Cure Autism?

47. Quoted in Julie Scelfo and Barbara Kantrowitz, "Families Cheer as Autism Bill Passes," *Newsweek*, October 15, 2007. www.newsweek.com.

48. Bill Blakemore, "Study Suggests Autism Causes Are Genetic," ABC News, February 18, 2007. http://abcnews.go.com.

49. Quoted in E.J. Mundell, "Major Gene Study Points to Causes of Autism," *Washington Post*, February 19, 2007. www.washingtonpost.com.

50. Quoted in Wallis, "Inside the Autistic Mind."

51. Quoted in NBC11.com, "Parents Credit Chelation with Autism Cure," March 3, 2006. www.nbc11.com.

52. Jim Adams, "Mercury, Chelation, and Autism," conference presentation, May 2007. http://autismone.org.

53. Quoted in National Institute of Mental Health, "New NIMH Research Program Launches Autism Trials," September 7, 2006. www.nimh.nih.gov.

54. Quoted in David Wolman, "The Truth About Autism: Scientists Reconsider What They *Think* They Know," *Wired*, February 25, 2008. www.wired.com.

55. Quoted in Wolman, "The Truth About Autism."

56. Kosloski, interview.

List of Illustrations

Index

About the Author

Peggy J. Parks holds a bachelor of science degree from Aquinas College in Grand Rapids, Michigan, where she graduated magna cum laude. She is an author who has written more than 70 nonfiction educational books for children and young adults, as well as self-published her own cookbook called *Welcome Home: Recipes, Memories, and Traditions from the Heart.* Parks lives in Muskegon, Michigan, a town that she says inspires her writing because of its location on the shores of Lake Michigan.